"Ernan Roman shows us how to listen to customers and improve our understanding of their preferences. This book is extremely valuable and provides a five-step process that guarantees higher revenue relationships with today's demanding customers."

Ida Rivière Le Quement,
Relationship Marketing Manager, Post Denmark

"Ernan's book is a must-read for marketing professionals in the for-profit and nonprofit sectors alike. The best practices he shares for acquiring and deepening relationships are invaluable."

Craig Kielburger, Founder, Free The Children

"Every marketer who values listening to and engaging with customers must read this. You are holding the key to the future in your hands."

Ole Stangerup, Chief Relationship Marketer, Express A/S

"Ernan and his team demonstrate a command of VOC research and how it can be used to transform an organization."

Colin Scully, Chairman & CEO, Life Line Screening

"Twenty-first-century marketing is in the midst of a revolution, and Ernan is leading it. This book is a must-read for those who refuse to be left behind."

Ichak Adizes, CEO and Founder, Adizes Institute

"Thank you, Ernan, for tuning us in to the inner voice of our customers! A deep understanding of our customers' needs and preferences is essential for our future growth."

Karen Galley, President, Patient News Publishing

"Ernan has done a masterful job of providing insights regarding how to work with today's consumers. The in-depth case studies provide valuable examples of customer-focused programs. He has given us much to think about and much to use."

Barrett Hazeltine, Professor of
Engineering Emeritus, Brown University

"As part of our commitment to Voice of the Customer, we realize we must build relationships first and do business second. Ernan's book provides essential guidelines for achieving high-quality customer engagement that brings loyalty and marketplace success."
Chris McCann, President, 1-800-FLOWERS.COM

"Ernan's 'Voice of the Customer' methodology provides an important guide for how to keep your finger on the pulse of your customers."
Yousef M. Hamidaddin, CEO,
Acxiom MENA & Arab DMA

"During difficult times, Ernan Roman is providing facts and figures on how the power of the VOC methodology and an integrated multimedia mix including direct mail will not only satisfy consumer demands but also produce double-digit results."
Pavlos Kamilos, Director,
Commercial Direction of Letter Mail,
Hellenic Post—ELTA

"The last word in implementing customer-focused best practices in today's complex multichannel world."
Akira Oka, President & CEO,
Direct Marketing Japan, Inc.

VOICE-OF-THE-CUSTOMER MARKETING

A REVOLUTIONARY FIVE-STEP PROCESS TO CREATE CUSTOMERS WHO CARE, SPEND, AND STAY

ERNAN ROMAN

New York   Chicago   San Francisco
Lisbon   London   Madrid   Mexico City
Milan   New Delhi   San Juan   Seoul
Singapore   Sydney   Toronto

1 2 3 4 5 6 7 8 9 10   DOC/DOC   1 8 7 6 5 4 3 2 1 0

ISBN   978-0-07-174083-8
MHID 0-07-174083-X

McGraw-Hill books are available at special quantity discounts to use as premiums and sales promotions or for use in corporate training programs. To contact a representative, please e-mail us at bulksales@mcgraw-hill.com.

This book is printed on acid-free paper.

*This book is dedicated with love to my wife Sheri,
the noblest Roman of us all, whose love, patience,
and good humor nurtured the birthing of this book
and the next generation of Roman marketers:
my daughter Helaina and son Elias and his wife Sarah,
who lovingly provided critiques of the manuscript
and insights regarding their world of social media.*

CONTENTS

IN A NUTSHELL: *By creating a process that allows organizations to engage with, listen to, and learn from customers and prospects, companies can harness the wisdom of the customer . . . and generate consistent double-digit increases in responses and sales.*

But there's a catch. To achieve those kinds of results, you must be willing to adopt a whole new vision of marketing. In this chapter, you learn why this book was written, and you get an overview of the five-step Voice-of-the-Customer (VOC) process.

STEP 1. Conduct and Apply VOC Relationship Research

IN A NUTSHELL: *The first step in the five-step process that connects a marketer to the wisdom of the customer calls for conducting VOC Relationship Research. This research is driven by in-depth interviews with customers and prospects.*

For instance: MSC Industrial Direct, a Fortune 1000 industrial supply company, identified competitively powerful strategies for strengthening relationships with customers and drove incremental sales in a "down" economy, using the VOC Relationship Research Process.

IN A NUTSHELL: *Palms Trading and Life Line Screening used VOC research to develop strategies for acquiring customers and achieving deeper, longer-lasting relationships with existing customers.*

You can use the VOC process in your own company to significantly deepen the level of engagement with your customers; gain new insights regarding what offers and/or services and messaging are relevant; understand what actions and/or experiences and messages will ensure significantly higher purchase and engagement rates; and identify gaps between the brand expectation and the reality of the purchase and service experience.

STEP 2. Create VOC-Driven Opt-In Relationship Strategies

IN A NUTSHELL: *True opt-in is about the relationship, not the first contact or first sale. An effective Opt-In/Self-Profiling Relationship Strategy begins the process of long-term engagement with the prospect or customer.*

Microsoft's online Business Resource Center is a best-in-class example of the VOC-driven opt-in relationship strategy. As this case study shows, simply firing off a few dozen self-profiling opt-in questions is not going to create a relationship. We must "earn the right": explain what information we're asking for, why we're asking for it, and how what we're planning to do with it benefits the other person.

IN A NUTSHELL: *Learn how establishing VOC-driven opt-in/self-profiling relationships with consumers will improve marketing results and establish a competitive advantage, for any company of any size in any industry.*

When you follow the guidelines outlined in this chapter, your opt-in process will enable you to identify, with great precision, exactly what value, services, and communications your customers want, and don't want, to receive from you. The Disney case study will show you how a master marketer ensures the delivery of relevant and targeted communications.

STEP 3. Create a VOC-Driven Multichannel Mix

IN A NUTSHELL: *Today's empowered consumers are demanding dramatic changes in their relationships with marketers. These consumers live in a multichannel world; many of the channels they choose are interactive.*

Aligning your organization's channel strategies with the preferences of your prospects and customers, as the Disney organization does, is one essential response to that change. So is synchronizing your message across channels. Today's consumers expect to be heard. The marketers who are willing to listen to them will establish a significant competitive edge.

IN A NUTSHELL: *Find additional real-world examples of how companies have listened closely to their customers and then used what they've learned to implement powerful multichannel programs.*
The case studies in this chapter illustrate how VOC-driven multichannel strategies can help organizations turn customers into evangelists (as Nike has proven); deliver 60 percent market share while competing with a global powerhouse (as SCA has achieved); and improve renewal rates by nearly 20 percent (as HMS National has proven).

STEP 4. Create a VOC-Driven Social Media Presence

IN A NUTSHELL: *Today, success in marketing is achieved as the result of a series of personal "conversations" and points of engagement with consumers and prospects. Ford Motor Company designed a social media–driven plan to create such engagements. Results were remarkable: 4.5 million YouTube views, 3.5 million Twitter impressions, and 80,000 "hand raisers" who asked to be kept up to date on the U.S. launch of the Ford Fiesta. Of all those hand raisers, 97 percent did not own a Ford vehicle.*
The Ford story demonstrates clearly that social media tools represent not a means for "selling" but rather a means for creating or improving relationships with consumers. Selling becomes a by-product of the quality and mutual benefit of those relationships.

IN A NUTSHELL: *The days of ignoring social media feedback about what your organization is doing are over. A successful social media strategy demands engagement, personalization, and effective targeting, as the case studies in this chapter prove.*

Engagement led online apparel retailer Threadless to 30 percent margins. Personalization allowed IBM to reposition itself with a critical target market of decision makers, generating a return visitor rate of 65 percent and a weekly rate of growth in the community of 10 percent. And sophisticated targeting using Google Ads has enabled the online customized stationery store Tiny Prints to turn profits since the year it was founded (2004).

IN A NUTSHELL: *Nonprofits and social businesses face a particularly sensitive set of tasks when it comes to deploying social media. Social media engagement with stakeholders must take place on a day-to-day, hour-to-hour, or even minute-to-minute basis. This level of connection is not only recommended for these organizations—it is now mandatory for success.*

Toronto-based Free The Children has built social media into its long-range strategic plan to free children from poverty and exploitation and (just as important) free young people from the notion that they are powerless to effect positive change in the world. California-based TOMS Shoes uses social media to win evangelists for its mission: for every pair of shoes it sells, TOMS gives a pair of shoes to a child in need. The company's ongoing feedback loop with customers also produces some of its best product ideas.

STEP 5. Invest in an Excellent Customer Service Experience

IN A NUTSHELL: *Customer service is a critical part of the marketing process. Your customers expect high-quality postsale support. If it is lacking, they will not only be inclined to go elsewhere but they will also be inclined to use the power of social media to let a lot of people know about their dissatisfaction!*

VOC-driven customer service is a strategic marketing differentiator that can ensure repeat business, higher rates of renewals, and more word-of-mouth recommendations. By recognizing the importance of customer service years ago and making it an integral part of its customer retention strategies, the innovative retailer QVC has built VOC-driven service into its business model—and established a powerful competitive advantage.

IN A NUTSHELL: *The way prospects and customers feel they have been treated by your company is the final, and best, test of whether your organization has in fact built itself around the Voice of the Customer. In this chapter, you get case studies from Comcast, 1-800-FLOWERS, and Disney proving that a VOC-driven customer service strategy can generate the internal and external "buzz" that makes it possible for organizations to pass the test.*

At the end of the day, companies don't change because of data. They change because of VOC stories, especially customer service stories.

IN A NUTSHELL: *The VOC Relationship Marketing Process requires organizational change. That is not easy. Begin by asking key stakeholders: "Whom do you serve?" For the total organization to listen to the Voice of the Customer, all entities of the organization must support each other and must determine who their internal or external clients are.*

The critical key performance indicator (KPI) that measures success in serving the respective customer is repeat purchases. Other KPIs specific to your industry and experience must also be developed and monitored; see the Appendix.

A recap of the most essential lessons.

Advice on what you should (and shouldn't) be measuring.

FOREWORD

Finally, someone has found the answer for how to succeed with customer-focused marketing. Ernan has pioneered an impressive Voice-of-the-Customer process that enables marketers to engage customers on their terms.

Today's companies spew out billions of communications every year. The tragedy is that the majority of these communications will have no impact whatsoever on most customers and prospects.

Consider all the promotions that find their way on to your computer screen that fail to engage you—or worse, irritate you. Consider all the catalogs that arrive in your mail that you immediately throw into the wastebasket. Consider all the phone calls that are meant to sell you something you have no interest in—and that you hang up on. Consider all the direct-mail campaigns that can barely reach a 1 percent response rate, which means that 99 percent of the messages were wasted.

All these communications have one thing in common: they are not relevant to you. These mass communications operate on a theory of large numbers. The assumption is that there will be enough hits among the ocean of misses to deliver a payoff.

Ernan Roman has proven, over and over again—in multiple industries, with companies huge and small, over nearly four decades—that there is a better way.

Appalled by the waste of client money and time, he has never stopped searching for new ways marketers can create increasingly relevant and long-lasting relationships with individual customers. His goal has always been to help marketers learn more about the needs of individual customers so they can provide increasingly relevant and targeted communications, aligned with the individual preferences of those customers and prospects.

Ernan has pioneered an impressive research-driven strategy process that is described in detail in this book. He uses in-depth Voice-of-the-Customer (VOC) Relationship Research to understand (a) how customers view the company and its products and communications and (b) what value propositions would be required to get these customers to "opt in" and self-profile their preferences, thus sharing valuable personal and business information. This opt-in information enables the marketer to send targeted and relevant information and offers that fit the preferences provided by the customers, using media that the customers themselves have chosen.

Ernan's consultancy has been retained by many of the major Fortune 100 companies—IBM, NBC Universal, Microsoft, Hewlett-Packard, and many others—based on his reputation for delivering powerful results. He has also helped smaller high-growth companies increase sales by developing strategies based on the true relationship needs of their customers and prospects.

He is justly proud of the results that his methodology has achieved in generating significant double-digit increases in sales, profits, customer retention, and satisfaction for his clients.

In this book, he shows how marketers can use these methods to improve response rates and revenue, strengthen their brands, and reduce tremendous levels of marketing waste.

All companies continually seek ways to create greater impact. The wrong way is to increase the volume of communications. The right way is to make communications more relevant and timely for each customer who receives them. Ernan has proven time and time again that the only way to engage effectively with customers is on their terms. His book offers a step-by-step guide for doing this the right way.

Philip Kotler
S.C. Johnson Distinguished Professor of
International Marketing
Kellogg School of Management
Northwestern University

PREFACE

Ernan Roman lives by a creed that too many corporate marketers forget:

Listen to your customer.

It's such a simple concept, but in practice, it is often ignored by businesses who just assume a product or service will attract tens of thousands of buyers. Actually, listening is the key.

I recall one of the first times I met Ernan. We were in a meeting about creating a series of new online services, and some colleagues were saying we should offer them this or give them that in exchange for the customers giving us key demographic data that would allow us to market to them more effectively. Ernan listened quietly for a bit and then asked, "Have you asked your customers whether they want this or not?" The room became quiet and I quietly chuckled.

Customers will tell you what they want. The trick is that companies sometimes forget to ask. And then, later, when the product fails miserably, the sales and marketing people wonder, "Where did we go wrong?"

Customers will tell you what you need to know, but you have to listen. They will give you vital personal information, such as their names, e-mail addresses, marital status, and more—if they can see the value in providing that information. I know I will, but I also know that I don't give out my information freely. As a consumer, I know I'm involved in a transaction, even if no money is involved. If I'm going to tell you where I live, what are you going to send me? If I tell you what magazines I read or TV shows I watch, how is that information going to improve the service you provide me?

My somewhat cynical and skeptical attitude as a consumer reflects the reality of many people in today's information-overloaded world. I know this not only from my own personal experience as a customer, but because many of my own company's customers have said so in research and through personal interviews. In other words, they told us. And we listened.

That's what Ernan's whole philosophy revolves around: getting customers to tell marketers like me what they want so we can create a better, more enduring business relationship. Customers are more than happy to tell businesses what they want. You just have to ask—and then really listen.

The return on your investment is worth it. Satisfied customers become loyal customers who buy more often and will spread the word to their friends and colleagues through word of mouth, online blogs, and influencer groups. They can become the evangelists for your business and its products or services. Conversely, dissatisfied customers can poison the well and keep others from ever considering you through those same online posts or customer reviews.

Ernan focuses on how we can create relationships with customers that allow us to contact those customers on a regular basis with new products, services, or promotions. In return, however, we must give something back. What we give back can take the form of tips, special discounts, product support, or maybe just access to a like-minded community. But if we don't give something to the relationship, the relationship will suffer. The trick is to find out what customers will find most valuable that you and your business can offer as an equitable trade.

Ernan's book helps you find out the key to creating a more targeted, effecting marketing campaign that has measurable sales results. Ernan calls it the "Voice of the Customer," and he uses a variety of creative techniques to elicit what customers really think about your products or services. Armed with this information, you can learn what you and your company need to do to improve sales and customer satisfaction. As Ernan has emphasized for years, the two are inextricably tied together.

Too many times, I have heard businesspeople ask, "Is your primary focus on driving revenue or customer satisfaction?" They are making a huge mistake because these are not mutually exclusive goals, but complementary. As Ernan has been teaching—and proving—for years, happier customers buy more and buy more often. Just ask them!

Eddie Yandle
Senior Director
Worldwide Small & Midmarket Solutions
& Partners
Microsoft Corporation

ACKNOWLEDGMENTS

This book is the result of collaborative relationships among three families.

First are the three generations of Romans who are direct marketers and have accumulated a remarkable body of experience and diverse perspectives. My father, Murray Roman, is acknowledged as the pioneer of the telemarketing industry, and he and my mother, Eva, introduced me to the world of high-value, person-to-person interactions. I am a second-generation marketer, and 37 years later, my fourth book on marketing best practices is the culmination of what I have learned thus far. My children represent the third generation of Romans with marketing in their DNA. Appropriate to their generation, their contributions are in the world of social media: Elias is the CEO of Songza Media, Inc., a social media–driven online music service, and my daughter, Helaina, is in affiliate marketing at BarnesandNoble.com. Our dinner conversations often sound like debates about multichannel marketing best practices.

The second family is composed of numerous clients who had the vision and courage to challenge traditional ways of thinking and retained us to help them transform the quality of the customer experience provided by their companies. There are hundreds of clients to whom I owe thanks. To avoid omitting any individual executives we've worked with, I will list the names of the companies who have been outstanding in their efforts to reengineer the quality of their marketing: Microsoft, IBM, NBC Universal, HMS Financial, Songza Media, Inc., Palms Trading, Walt Disney, MSC Industrial Direct, Life Line Screening, Hewlett-Packard, and many others.

The third family is made up of valued industry colleagues who have taught me so much. The first call-out goes to the Direct Marketing Association (DMA) whose support over many decades has meant a great deal. The DMA has encouraged innovation and collegial information sharing between all the generations of marketers—old-timers, newcomers, traditional marketers, and digital marketers—across all industries.

They supported my new methodologies and provided forums to share these best practices worldwide. My gratitude and appreciation of the Direct Marketing Association's CEOs and staff over the years is profound. A special thanks to Paul McDonnough, Sue Geramian, and Lisa Merizio-Smith for their support, guidance, and friendship.

Another branch of the family of industry colleagues are the many peers I've had the honor to work with and learn from and with whom I have exchanged ideas, war stories, and many good times. And above all, we have shared the common goal of propelling our industry to the highest levels of excellence and innovation.

A special call-out also goes to Brandon Yusuf Toropov, who was a wonderful help in developing this book.

Also, heartfelt thanks go to every single member of my wonderful team at Ernan Roman Direct Marketing for your professionalism, dedication, and the value you provide to our clients.

To the individual clients, colleagues, and employees referenced above, I say: thank you, thank you, thank you.

A final note of appreciation for a special group of people. The quality of this book was immeasurably improved by the Voice-of-the-Customer feedback from a dedicated circle of colleagues. In spite of heavy workloads, they made the time to provide thorough reviews and detailed, candid critiques of the early drafts of the book. Heartfelt thanks go to Rich Bonfiglio, Lisa Clawson, Garry Dawson, Professor Barrett Hazeltine, Marc Horowitz, Marnie Kittelson, Professor Philip Kotler, Professor Harvey Markowitz, Fred Neil, Don Peppers, Leslie Reiser, Elias Roman, Helaina Roman, Sarah Roman, Sheri Roman, Ole Stangerup, Doug Stein, and Eddie Yandle.

INTRODUCTION

THE VISION FOR VOC-DRIVEN MARKETING

In a time when everything we know as marketers seems subject to instant change—a time of social media explosions and 24/7 connectivity and demographic shifts of seemingly infinite complexity—there remains one and only one factor that marketers can count on: the wisdom of the customer. The question is, how do we tap into that wisdom?

This book is the culmination of 37 years in the marketing trenches. In that time I have had the privilege of helping a wide range of companies, from IBM, Microsoft, and NBC Universal, to MSC Industrial Direct, to Palms Trading, one of the oldest Native American trading posts.

The executives and entrepreneurs in these companies and hundreds of others all had one trait in common: they were not willing to accept traditional marketing tactics that blast out undifferentiated e-mail, mail, phone calls, and other messages for obscenely poor returns on their marketing investment. (I call this "spray-and-pray marketing.")

These executives realized that in no other part of their business would they tolerate a 0.25 percent response rate, or perhaps, on a good day, a 1 percent response rate. In no other part of their business would they consider it appropriate to throw away 99 percent of their effort—and celebrate a 99 percent failure rate.

They also realized that, in today's environment, response rates would continue to worsen as buyers became better informed, thanks to the astonishing array of options and information available to them via the Internet. They knew too that consumers would be more inclined than ever to "opt out" of annoying or irrelevant marketing communications.

The entrepreneurs I worked with knew there had to be a better way to reach consumers. They trusted me to deliver on the promise of a disciplined marketing process, a process that tapped into the wisdom of the customer and engaged people to opt in to, rather than opt out of, relationships with marketers.

I've learned firsthand that, by creating a process that allows organizations to engage with, listen to, and learn from customers and prospects, companies can harness the wisdom of the customer . . . and generate consistent *double-digit increases in responses and sales.*

But there's a catch. To achieve those kinds of results, you must be willing to adopt a whole new vision of marketing.

This book was written to fulfill such a vision.

The vision is that we can transform the discipline of marketing by finding a way to engage our customers on their own terms and by being truly consumer focused. That we can treat customers the way we ourselves want to be treated when we make a purchase decision. That we can find a way to do what we all know, deep down inside, is the right thing for the consumer. By the way, when I say "we," I'm referring not only to my own team at Ernan Roman Direct Marketing but also to all the clients who have used the principles outlined in this book and who have taken part in the intensive process that helped me to create and improve its contents for you.

The vision that drives this book is that we can follow our own best intuitions about the way the art and science of marketing should be pursued in the twenty-first century . . . and that we can meet or exceed our financial objectives by doing right by customers and prospects.

The vision is that we can somehow, at long last, find a way to allow our own expectations of the marketing process, born from our own personal experiences as consumers, to drive the experiences we ourselves deliver to consumers.

And as if all of that weren't enough, the vision goes further. It demands that, in doing all of this, we pay no bottom-line price but rather experience dramatic *double-digit improvements* over what we have been doing up to this point.

This vision is not fantasy. It's what some of the most successful organizations in the world are experiencing right now. It's what we all could be experiencing. The vision is rooted in a principle known as *Voice of the Customer*, or VOC for short.

VOC-ABULARY

"VOC" is the *Voice of the Customer*—a term used to describe the process of capturing critical details regarding the desires, needs, and requirements of a given prospect, customer, or target group. VOC is both a way of looking at marketing and a specialized research methodology. VOC yields an in-depth understanding of customer and prospect preferences and actions—the kind of understanding that the marketer can use to develop powerful relationship marketing and engagement strategies. VOC is what allows us to give customers what they really want most from us— and avoid the annoyance and alienation that results from offering them what they don't want.

The process that turns this vision into reality is a battle-tested, relationship-focused five-step system that gets us closer to the customer, treats the customer as we ourselves would want to be treated, and keeps the customer engaged with us as we navigate changes in technology, markets, and media—together. The benefits of adopting this customer-driven discipline are compelling: dramatically increased short- and long-term revenue, increased customer lifetime value and loyalty, and in this age of social media, greater advocacy for your brand where it matters: on the front lines. The cost of *ignoring* this five-step process is equally stark: increasing customer alienation, increased numbers of people opting out of your communications, and long-term damage to your brand that, all too often, goes unnoticed until it is too late to repair the damage.

In recent years, there have been many customer relationship management (CRM) initiatives that have not listened well to the Voice of the Customer. As well intentioned as these initiatives have been, we must acknowledge that today's customers do not feel like being "managed" (or, for that matter, manipulated). Going forward, the premise of marketing and indeed the entire enterprise must begin **not** with the idea of "managing" relationships—as we might "manage" a crisis or "manage" risk. Rather, we must begin with the vision of creating a community in which customers know their voice is being heard and acted on and in which they therefore look forward to engaging with us because they derive value from doing so.

The five steps that allow us to engage customers in this way are illustrated below. Notice that the first step, Voice of Customer, drives the subsequent four steps and that all five steps are interrelated.

STEP 1.
CONDUCT AND APPLY VOC RELATIONSHIP RESEARCH

This involves in-depth interviews with prospects, customers, and key stakeholders to understand how they expect the marketer to satisfy their needs for a high-value relationship that includes increasingly relevant offers, services, and communications.

By doing this, MSC Industrial Direct, a Fortune 1000 industrial supply company, was able to:

- Avoid investing time and resources in a campaign to "win back" customers who had not really left at all, but instead had changed their buying patterns.
- Develop competitively powerful strategies for strengthening relationships with high-value customers.
- Identify significant opportunities to drive incremental sales among critical customer segments.

STEP 2.
CREATE VOC-DRIVEN OPT-IN RELATIONSHIP STRATEGIES

This means engaging prospects and consumers to tell you exactly what they value and want from you . . . and what they don't want from you.

By creating an opt-in relationship marketing program, software giant Microsoft experienced the following "unprecedented" results:

- Opt-in rates that range between 45 to 95 percent
- Response rates that are currently performing in the *double digits*
- Revenue that is expected to continue being significantly greater than the revenue from the control population

STEP 3.
CREATE A VOC-DRIVEN MULTICHANNEL MIX

This means creating an integrated, multichannel marketing program that engages and inspires your customer.

The Walt Disney Companies created such a program for its resort operations. As a result, Disney has achieved the following:

- Grown the database by over 100 percent
- Increased the number of targeted interactions by over 10 times
- Expanded e-mail coverage by over 10 times

STEP 4.
CREATE A VOC-DRIVEN SOCIAL MEDIA PRESENCE

This means creating strategies for real-time engagement with your customers and prospects.

By doing this, Ford Motor Company not only took control of a public relations crisis but also generated the following:

- 4.5 million YouTube views
- 3.5 million Twitter impressions
- 80,000 "hand raisers" who asked to be kept up to date on the U.S. launch of the Ford Fiesta (A staggering 97 percent of the hand raisers did not own a Ford vehicle.)

STEP 5.
INVEST IN AN EXCELLENT CUSTOMER SERVICE EXPERIENCE

This means not pretending that customer service is something for operations to worry about.

By building this philosophy into its corporate culture, QVC experienced the following:

- 20 percent reduction in complaints and/or queries from customers
- 93 percent repurchase rate among the most satisfied customers

These companies prove that the VOC-driven vision is attainable and drives remarkable increases in revenue. I believe we all should be striving to attain this level of excellence—no matter how "customer centric" we consider our organizations to be right now.

Social media facilitate and accelerate this level of customer engagement. This phenomenon has changed forever the field upon which all marketers must play. The constantly shifting channel mix, trending inevitably toward more and more personalized engagement, could not have happened at a better time.

Social media are first and foremost media that reach their recipients on the recipients' terms—meaning that information must get past a certain set of filters that the prospect or customer has deliberately applied over time. The difference between traditional messaging and social media messaging might thus be compared to the difference between buying a new pair of sneakers based on a TV ad versus buying it based on a recommendation tweeted by an NBA player whom you follow on Twitter. One involves a passive spray-and-pray approach; the other involves direct, active engagement with people one knows and trusts. As we shall see in later chapters, the difference is significant, and it has rocked the marketing world (in a very positive way).

More and more information is getting to users in this highly personalized, highly filtered way. That means less and less traditional marketing information is going to reach users via the traditional routes. For marketers, the implication is that ever fewer users are reachable through the traditional channels that allow *us* to select *them*—and ever more users are reachable only via the user-filtered sources that allow *them* to "follow" *us*.

We marketers are experiencing these changes firsthand. Today, each of us operates his or her own network of networks. Whether that meta-network comprises bloggers, friends on Facebook, people or companies we follow on Twitter, and/or videos we watch on YouTube, we will opt in to it, and we will use the meta-network as a filter—that is, as a kind of gatekeeper—to determine what information reaches us and what doesn't.

The five steps detailed in this book will show you how to succeed in getting today's empowered consumers to embrace you as an integral part of that meta-network.

In the next part of the book, we'll begin looking at Step 1 of the process.

CONDUCT AND APPLY VOC RELATIONSHIP RESEARCH

CHAPTER 1

CONDUCT VOC RELATIONSHIP RESEARCH

EXECUTIVE SUMMARY

- The first step in the five-step process that connects a marketer to the wisdom of the customer calls for conducting VOC Relationship Research. This foundational research is driven by in-depth interviews with customers and prospects.
- MSC Industrial Direct, a Fortune 1000 industrial supply company, identified competitively powerful strategies for strengthening relationships with customers and driving incremental sales using the VOC Relationship Research Process.

To turn customer feedback into an organizational asset, we must do more than send out simple surveys based on what we think the most important business issues of the day are. We must make listening to, analyzing, and taking action on the Voice of the Customer an organizational priority. The listening must take place on an ongoing basis, in response to specific customer experiences. It must also take place on the basis of what my colleague Don Peppers refers to as "pulse monitoring"—that is, a systematic series of direct engagements with customers and other stakeholders designed to capture detailed reactions.

WHAT IS VOC RELATIONSHIP RESEARCH?

The VOC Relationship Research Process has been refined over a period of 20 years, by means of over 125 research studies representing over 10,000 hours of interviews.

The focus of most of these in-depth research efforts has been to identify actionable market intelligence that defines strategies for *significantly increasing revenue*—by better understanding customers. A deeper understanding of your customers will inevitably increase your likelihood of winning:

- More customers
- Customers with greater loyalty
- Powerful word-of-mouth referrals

VOC guidance enables you to achieve greater Customer Lifetime Value through the following:

- Increased sales of new and existing products and/or services
- The development of more effective value propositions and messaging
- The creation of powerful "call-to-action" triggers
- The deployment of an integrated multichannel mix *based on customer preferences*
- The development of effective *and appropriate* Opt-In/Self-Profiling Strategies
- Reduction in wasted time and money spent on ineffective marketing initiatives

This process can be applied to any company. The results of companies profiled in this book—Microsoft, IBM, MSC Industrial Direct, Palms Trading, and many others—prove that VOC insights can help large and small companies in technology, software, media and entertainment, heavy industry, hospitality, energy, and virtually every other sector of the global economy.

VOC Relationship Research improves your marketing by uncovering in-depth marketing information that answers critical questions such as these:

- How do customers view the strengths and weaknesses of your company?
- Do your customers feel that your company is providing the value they expected?
- What do customers expect from you in a deeper, competitively differentiating relationship?
- What are the critical issues facing decision makers as they evaluate your product or service?
- What are the reactions of customers and prospects to your messages, tactics, and offers?
- How do customers define their unique messaging and information requirements?
- How do customers define the parameters for an opt-in/self-profiling, preference-driven relationship with your company? (You'll learn more about this kind of relationship in Step 2.)
- What questions are appropriate to ask a prospect or customer as part of the opt-in/self-profiling process? And when is it appropriate to ask them to opt in and self-profile in the course of their relationship life cycle with your company?
- How long does the decision-making process take, and who are the critical decision makers and influencers?
- What information is required at each step and via what mix of media?
- What is the optimal value-added role for sales channels?

VOC also helps you to do the following:

- Change from a relationship based on transactions between you and your customers to a deeper engagement based on your deeper understanding of their needs.
- Understand the critical issues facing decision makers as they evaluate your product or service.
- Understand the steps in the decision-making process.
- Identify the likely decision makers and the empowered influencers.
- Determine what information and offers are most effective at each step of the sales process, and via what mix of channels.

- Determine the optimal role for the following:
  - Social media
  - Internet
  - E-mail
  - Direct mail
  - Inside sales and inbound/outbound telemarketing
  - Field sales
  - Tech support
  - Stores

The VOC Relationship Research Process helps you develop powerful and actionable strategies and tactics as a result of in-depth, one-to-one—voice-to-voice or face-to-face—interviews, typically lasting one hour. These interviews are not your organization's only sources of information about what your customers expect from you, but they are an essential starting point.

Our company started with face-to-face interviews, and we continued them for years. Eventually, however, we changed to telephone interviews due to feedback we received from interviewees during VOC research programs we were conducting for clients. People we were interviewing face-to-face told us that phone interviews were less intrusive and more convenient. Switching to telephone interviews meant that we could eliminate travel costs, complete the research more quickly for our clients, and still have the benefit of the in-depth hour-long research interviews.

Companies use these in-depth VOC insights as internal marketing road maps—and, not infrequently, they also use them as authoritative argument settlers when internal turf or political conflicts threaten to take organizations off track.

Increasingly, we've seen that when organizations make changes that profoundly improve their strategic and competitive positions, they do so because of something they have learned or stories they have heard directly from the mouths of their customers.

The competitive advantages of the information that results from VOC research are game changing, but those benefits will not materialize unless you follow a specific process that will ensure you are asking the right questions for the right reasons. That process is the subject of this chapter.

COMMON OBJECTIONS TO CONDUCTING VOC RESEARCH

Among the objections we sometimes hear from companies who resist conducting VOC research are these:

- Customers don't say what they mean. They say one thing and do another.
- We already did this. We talked to customers at our [trade show/ annual meeting/other gathering], and we didn't really get anything we didn't already know.
- I talked to our best customer last night and got all the feedback I need.
- Keeping in touch with our customers is a key reason we have salespeople. Isn't that enough?
- Why can't we just send a letter asking for written feedback?
- Why can't we just send out an online survey?

We have learned empirically that customers *do* know what they want and are happy to take advantage of opportunities to tell marketers what they want. The problem often lies with the companies: companies don't always ask the right questions, don't always listen to what the customers are actually saying, and don't always like the answers they get when they do, but that's another matter.

As for gathering off-the-cuff insights at trade shows and other venues, this is fine for anecdotal information. But keep in mind that this does not and cannot take the place of disciplined, systematic, in-depth discussions with customers.

Online surveys have their place, and they are certainly very easy to administer. The fact is, however, that they often do not yield the *depth of insight* required to drive new solutions to the strategic challenges we face. Too often, surveys tend to reinforce our preconceptions rather than challenge them.

If our goal is to find out how and why the competition is securing a larger portion of a customer's total budget than we are, for instance, we should probably begin by acknowledging that we *don't know what we don't know* about that customer's personal and operational experiences with us. These are likely to be important gaps that are well beyond our current experience base, and we need to pose open-ended questions and engage in in-depth conversations if we hope to fill those gaps.

This is not to say that online surveys and other quantitative tools can't be effective in helping us determine what's working or what's not. They can, but it is often necessary for us to go much deeper than these tools are designed to go.

IN-DEPTH INTERVIEWS: POWERFUL TOOLS FOR MARKETERS
Marnie Kittelson, Research and Marketing Expert

In-depth interviews, commonly referred to as IDIs, are an essential tool in any marketer's toolbox. Basically, in-depth interviewing is a research method that uses open-ended questions to elicit perceptions, thoughts, and feelings on a specific topic of interest, and it allows interviewees to express these opinions in their own words. IDIs can be conducted in any type of setting that offers an intimate connection between interviewer and interviewee—most often face-to-face or voice-to-voice via telephone. However, with the technological evolution, the industry is seeing Webcam IDIs becoming more popular, and we expect there will be even more ways to conduct these types of interviews in the near future.

The beauty of using this type of research is that it uncovers the "whys" of a particular marketing or business issue. It's easy enough to get at the "what's" of a problem—anyone can fire off a Survey Monkey e-mail laden with "How would you rate . . ." and "Which statement best describes . . ." questions that get you only to the realization that a problem exists, not what's causing it.

Because the interview is conducted one-on-one, there is no social pressure, no "group think"—just one consumer talking about his or her experiences with one trained interviewer. An experienced interviewer will establish a rapport with the interviewee, guide him or her through the preselected questions, but then probe and delve into areas that offer greater insights or different perceptions than were expected. This level of nuance, laced with rich descriptive details, is the real value of an IDI—finding the information you didn't even know you didn't know.

Engaging customers in a conversation where they feel comfortable talking about the business environment they are dealing with and how your company affects it, the particular challenges they are facing, and even how they want to connect with your company provides information that marketers can't get with other marketing or research methodologies. Other methods might (or might not) be able to "check the pulse" of your customers, but IDIs will tell you what will get their heart racing.

Ultimately, IDIs offer marketers the ability to hear their customers' stories, told from their points of view, with their own words. It's then your job to listen and apply these learnings.

HOW TO ESTABLISH THE CORRECT OBJECTIVES THAT WILL DRIVE THE VOC RESEARCH

Effective VOC Relationship Research depends on a number of elements. The first and arguably most important element is the identification of the right objectives.

The products and services developed by marketers don't always connect with the true needs of their customers or prospects. The VOC provides an in-depth understanding of the straight line toward the "true North" that is the wisdom of the customer.

To help you in finding this true North, the objectives that drive effective VOC Relationship Research must be:

1. Generated and evaluated by a cross-functional team, so the VOC will reflect the needs of the major stakeholders
2. Strategically sound and in alignment with the goals of senior management
3. Based on the unique conditions faced by your organization and your customer segments

Consider all three of these requirements nonnegotiable. Fulfilling them takes time. Given the complexity and importance of these three requirements, it's a virtual certainty that the right objectives for your research campaign are *not* what tumble out of your mouth instantly the moment you start talking about what you'd like to learn from, and about, your customers or prospects.

WRITE CLEAR OBJECTIVES AND INTERVIEW QUESTIONS

- Define a clear set of issues or opportunities, and develop a concise set of VOC research objectives to address these specific issues.
- Do not define your objectives too broadly. Stay focused on the major issues at hand so you'll gain an in-depth understanding—and be able to develop the strategies and action items that can improve customer experiences.
- Don't create too many objectives because each objective will require a number of questions in the Interview Guide. If you end up with too many questions, you will lose the value of the in-depth discussions and insights that the VOC Relationship Research provides.
- Create questions that involve and engage participants, and challenge them to think. For instance, instead of simply asking, "How likely would you be to recommend our service to friends and family?" you might want to ask, "What improvements would you need to see to be comfortable enough to recommend our product or service to a friend?"

It takes a great deal of thought and discussion to determine the right objectives for VOC Relationship Research. You'll know you're dealing with good candidates for your campaign's research objectives when they touch on one or more of these four strategic marketing imperatives:

- Attracting prospects
- Converting prospects to customers

- Selling more to existing customers through better levels of engagement and value
- Keeping the customers you've got

If something points you toward how one or more of these four strategic imperatives is actually happening right now—what's keeping one or more of them from happening, or what could allow one or more of these four factors to happen more profitably and efficiently in the future—you're looking at a potential objective for your VOC Relationship Research effort.

To demonstrate how this first essential step of the VOC process works, let's review the following case study.

CASE STUDY:
THE VOC IN THE INDUSTRIAL WORLD—
MSC INDUSTRIAL DIRECT

CLOSE-UP ON MSC INDUSTRIAL DIRECT
- Founded in 1941
- One of the nation's leading distributors of metalworking and maintenance, repair, and operations (MRO) industrial supplies
- Offers over 600,000 products
- www.mscdirect.com

MSC Industrial Direct is a Fortune 1000 industrial supply company founded in 1941. Like all the companies whose case studies we are sharing with you in this book, MSC has customers it must keep satisfied and loyal, and it faces real and ever-shifting market challenges in doing so.

To resolve some of those challenges, MSC began by adopting a core principle of this book: in times of rapid market change, the wisdom of the customer is the only reliable constant. While MSC prides itself on staying close to its customers and employs many methods to capture customer feedback, senior management at MSC decided it was time to ask customers for guidance and help in a manner that would provide the most unbiased information.

To understand the company's decision, you will need a little background. MSC distributes over 600,000 items to a broad, diverse base of customers that range from small manufacturing companies to Fortune 1000 companies—as well as customers at many state and federal government accounts. MSC reaches its many customers through a variety of sales channels: direct mail, outside salespeople, telesales, and the Internet.

As Rich Bonfiglio, director of customer marketing at MSC, explained: "Culturally, MSC's internal priorities are clear: the primary goal, up and down the organization, for everyone from senior executives to frontline associates, is to provide an extremely high level of focus on providing exceptional service to every customer, on every order."

Many companies claim to have this kind of customer-focused culture, of course, but MSC's actions in the marketplace show that MSC does in fact walk its talk: customer feedback is solicited at every level, in formats ranging from online and telephone surveys, to discussions with direct salespeople, to one-on-one contacts with the CEO.

Given MSC's culturally reinforced connection to its customer base, and its willingness to reach out in many media and listen to what it heard, one might have been tempted to conclude that the company "didn't need" VOC research. That, however, would have been a mistake, because the challenge MSC faced was not one that could be resolved with a survey or even by a call or two from the CEO.

Why Conduct VOC Relationship Research?

According to Rich, "The recession that bogged down the United States (and indeed the global) economy beginning in late 2008 brought about a major change in a specific, and significant, segment of the MSC customer base. The problem was that buyers in this segment abruptly changed their purchasing pattern."

Unlike many companies that faced the challenge of adjusting to the grim realities of the recession, MSC didn't begin by assuming that it already knew the answer to those questions. Instead, management worked from the assumption that they *didn't* know.

"The easy response we could have used to explain what was happening," Rich told us, "was the answer that seemed the most obvious: the overall economic landscape was causing customers to stop placing orders with us. The problem with that explanation, though, was that other customer segments were not exhibiting the same degree of change in behavior. If the recession really was the most important factor affecting purchases, it should have been affecting all of our customer groups roughly equally. Clearly, it wasn't. So we knew we had some research to do. We needed to know what was really happening, whether we were losing customers to the competition, and, if so, where were they going and why."

Quantitative customer surveys conducted internally by MSC indicated no issues related to product availability, pricing, or service. Both purchasing and nonpurchasing customers had the same high regard for MSC.

This data raised the question: If customers were satisfied with MSC, why were some of the customers buying so much less than others?

Developing and Planning the VOC Relationship Research

Here are the guidelines we used to help MSC develop objectives that would drive the VOC Relationship Research.

- Define a clear set of issues or opportunities, and develop a concise set of VOC research objectives to address these specific issues.
- Do not define your objectives too broadly. Stay focused on the issue at hand so you'll gain an in-depth understanding and therefore be able to develop actionable strategies and action items.
- Don't create too many objectives; each objective will require a number of questions in the Interview Guide. If you end up with too many questions, you will lose the value of the in-depth discussions and insights that the VOC Relationship Research provides.

In accordance with these guidelines, the following objectives were defined for the MSC VOC research:

1. Determine the impact of the economy on spending in the target segment.
2. Identify the factors that drive "When to buy."
3. Identify the factors that drive "What to buy."
4. Identify the factors that affect "Whom" (which companies) the people in this segment buy from.
5. Determine whether any suppliers receive the majority of the customers' orders and why.

These were the driving challenges that the VOC research had to address. These were the *objectives* of the VOC. A solid VOC research project typically has between 5 and 10 objectives.

Two important tests of VOC objectives are these: Do the objectives we've identified lead us toward important business questions that customers and prospects care about answering? And, once we know these answers, will we be able to act on them?

Whom Should We Interview?

Another essential step is to identify the research sample.

Once they know the objectives, many executives (and particularly company founders) are eager to get started by reaching for the phone: *Let's start getting the answers right now!*

There is a problem with this approach. Simply identifying the top-tier objectives, and creating the questions driven by those objectives, does not mean we are ready to begin our VOC research. We still do not have two essential components: the people we want to target for the interviews and the structured questions we want to ask those people.

DON'T REACH FOR THE PHONE YET!

Simply calling your "best customers"—that is, those customers with whom you or someone in your organization already has a productive one-on-one relationship—is not VOC Relationship Research.

Setting up the "research grid" is the essential next step. Within this grid, you must identify the specific *target groups* whose guidance and help will allow you to answer the questions you've posed, and you must decide on the number of interviews you wish to hold with each.

Carefully developing the grid for your VOC research is a critical part of the process whose importance cannot be overstated. The groups you identify must reflect the critical business objectives of your organization. In order for that to happen, you must begin a comprehensive internal conversation within your organization.

This conversation, which should include key stakeholders from throughout the enterprise, must have the goal of determining the most important customer and prospect constituencies—the groups and sub-groups that will enable you to move forward in meeting your objectives. Failing to hold these conversations means you are assuming that all your key constituencies are more or less identical. Treating all customers and prospects as essentially identical is a classic (and expensive) mistake that will inevitably lead you down blind alleys, waste time and money, and undermine your organization's efforts to get actionable help, guidance, and market intelligence from your VOC research.

START BUILDING AN INTERNAL COALITION FOR CHANGE

Include people from a variety of departments, with a variety of functional backgrounds, in your discussions about objectives, questions, and research sample groups. Be sure to include a mix of senior-level people (who will help to focus the discussion) and midlevel people (whose buy-in will be essential when it comes time to implement the new initiatives arising from the VOC research). This is important because the proposed changes that arise from these initiatives are often dramatic.

Make sure the population of prospects, contacts, and customers you're targeting is one you can actually extract from your database when it comes time to implement the new strategies identified by your VOC research. If you spend all of your time and energy talking to the "blue" people within your customer base, but you can't pull out "blue" users when you want to roll out your new program, you will have simply wasted your resources. The groups and subgroups you select must reflect what you can segment—and act on—in your database.

Determining How Many People to Interview and How Much Time the Interviews Should Take

Identifying the most critical customer and prospect constituencies is only the beginning. You must also determine *how many* people within each subgroup you should interview. As a general rule, we have found that eight is the ideal number of interviews per subgroup. This provides eight hours of in-depth insights from each subgroup. When this data is aggregated with that of the other subgroups, we have found that this sample size is sufficient to support good decision making. Bear in mind, though, that you are not trying to gather a "statistically significant sample" of any group, as you would if you were conducting quantitative research. The results of these discussions are meant to provide a Voice-of-the-Customer understanding—which means understanding real-world perceptions and expectations among prospects and customers. These insights are what we need to develop customer-focused marketing strategies and action plans.

During the planning process for this VOC research, Rich understood the importance of selecting the right research sample. "You have to put as much work into developing the customer lists to be utilized in the research as you put into developing the objectives and questions," he advised. "I cannot overemphasize this. The datasets chosen must be as accurate a cross section of the customer base as possible in order for the results to be valid. In our case, we were focused on a specific segment of the customer base; below that segment were subsegments that pertained to how the customers were serviced, their level of sales activity, and the recency of their last purchase. This ultimately yielded a total of 12 datasets to be targeted during our interviews."

Rich offered this advice for anyone attempting to conduct this kind of in-depth research: "Scrub your lists to the *n*th degree! For example, if customers can open several accounts with you, spend time determining whether any of the accounts you are probing are tied to any other accounts. There's nothing more embarrassing than asking a customer why she hasn't purchased only to find out that she bought yesterday under another account."

What Should We Ask?

The five MSC objectives, and the selection of the right research sample, led MSC to the next major step: an initial draft of survey questions, some with subquestions, all of which were gathered into a document called an Interview Guide.

In keeping with the principles we've shared in this chapter, a cross-functional team participated in the process of developing this critical document. Sales was brought in from the start and asked to participate in developing the questions, but as the project progressed, stakeholders from other key areas such as marketing, advertising, logistics, customer service, and e-commerce were involved in the VOC process. To get the fullest possible sense of the customers' experience, this team created both qualitative and quantitative questions.

Quantitative questions are those whose answers can be counted and compiled, such as "How many widgets does your company use right now?" Qualitative questions, on the other hand, generate responses that are subjective, more in-depth, and more nuanced: "Speaking on a personal level, what was your biggest challenge when it came to learning to use widgets?" You need a good discussion to generate the right questions in each category. In MSC's case, members of the sales team were important early contributors to that discussion.

"There were two big reasons to bring in the sales team early on in the process," Rich pointed out. "First, people who work in areas closest to the issue at hand can often add invaluable insights when it comes to framing the questions and anticipating the responses. Second, and just as important, we knew that gaining buy-in from the sales team up front would help us gain acceptance of the results that came back from the project."

Two critical points on Interview Guide content are worth mentioning here. First, the questions in the Interview Guide must be clearly driven by the objectives. Extraneous "nice-to-know" questions must be discarded.

Second, the list of questions you develop is a starting point for the conversation with each person you are interviewing, not an ending point. In other words, this is not a checklist. Just as a skilled interviewer in a job interview setting must do, you must be prepared to explore relevant new ideas, concerns, data points, and insights as they are mentioned by interviewees. If the questions you create do not help you probe and understand each interviewee's unique perspective and his or her positive or negative experiences with your organization, then you must revise and improve the list of questions. Get input from multiple stakeholders on the relevance and phrasing of the questions. For instance, get input from the owner and/or founder of the company, the head of sales, the three best customers you have, and the head of customer service.

So, who should conduct the interviews? You want seasoned, tested people with research experience who understand the business and marketing objectives of your business so they can identify potential opportunities shared by interviewees and deeply probe these for meaningful insights and action items. You may want to consider a rotating system that includes interviewers from each department or work group that will eventually be responsible for *implementing* the initiatives that will be derived from the VOC research. This increases internal buy-in.

As mentioned earlier, our experience from conducting over 125 VOC research projects has demonstrated that eight hours of interviews per each carefully selected cell is sufficient to generate the depth of information required. Think of how much you can learn from 50 or 60 hours of carefully structured and focused conversations from key customer and prospect segments!

The empirical experiences of hundreds of companies who have conducted VOC research prove that a small number of in-depth, carefully structured interviews with customers and prospects can indeed yield invaluable insights.

Of course, each of these interviews represents a significant investment of time, resources, and energy. The good news about that investment, however, is that once you make it, you will have gleaned critical, and very often, game-changing insights about your market *as a whole*— all from a seemingly tiny number of discussions with consumers!

In the questionnaire that appears on pages 27–29 is a sampling of MSC's research questions. They were driven by both the objectives

(continues on page 29)

ERNAN ROMAN DIRECT MARKETING

I. Background Information

1. What's been the impact of the economy on your company within the past 12 to 18 months?
2. Has this resulted in:
   - ☐ Reduced head count
   - ☐ Reduced work hours
   - ☐ Complete shutdowns (holiday shutdown, summer shutdown, and so on)
   - ☐ Something else. Specify: _____

II. Purchase Procedures

I'd like to understand how your company makes industrial supply purchases:

3. What role do you play in the decision to purchase industrial supplies?
4. Could you walk me through the purchase process? What are the steps?
5. Has the purchasing process changed in the past 12 to 18 months?

III. Deciding Whom to Buy From

6. Below is a list of factors you might consider when deciding from whom to purchase industrial supplies. Please select the five most important items and rank them in importance. Please rank the most important item number 1, the second most important number 2, and so on, until you have ranked the top five factors:
   - ___ Credit policy and payment terms
   - ___ Financial stability of supplier

___ Highly personalized service and communications
___ In-person sales representatives
___ Next-day delivery
___ Pricing
___ Same-day delivery
___ Shipping cost
___ Supplier's on-hand inventory
___ Telephone sales representatives
___ Something else. Specify: _____

7. Has what you think about when deciding from whom to purchase industrial supplies changed in the past 12 to 18 months?

IV. Suppliers

8. From what companies do you buy industrial supplies?
   ☐ Competitor A
   ☐ Competitor B
   ☐ Competitor C
   ☐ MSC
   ☐ Local suppliers
   ☐ Other. Specify: _____

9. Roughly, what percent of your purchases comes from each supplier you mentioned?
   ☐ Competitor A
   ☐ Competitor B
   ☐ Competitor C
   ☐ MSC
   ☐ Local suppliers
   ☐ Other. Specify: _____

10. Why do you distribute your purchases that way?

11. Has your company's distribution of purchases changed from the past? In other words, have you changed the percentage of purchases you make from different suppliers?

12. For each of the top five attributes you identified in Section III, how does MSC compare to the supplier you use most often?

If MSC is the supplier you use most often, please compare it to the supplier you use next most frequently. If you have more than one supplier that you use most often, please compare MSC to each of your top two suppliers.

	Better Than	As Good As	Worse Than
Attribute ranked 1	☐	☐	☐
Attribute ranked 2	☐	☐	☐
Attribute ranked 3	☐	☐	☐
Attribute ranked 4	☐	☐	☐
Attribute ranked 5	☐	☐	☐

V. MSC

13. Relative to other companies you order from, what are the strengths of MSC?
14. Relative to other companies you order from, what are the weaknesses of MSC?

outlined above and by the input from the cross-functional team. Notice that this is a *broad outline* of questions to be covered during the interview and that many of the questions are open ended, allowing the interviewer to focus on the specific stories, insights, and challenges of individual interviewees. Like the MSC team, you must invest the time, effort, and energy necessary to create a similarly flexible question set that enables you to support a conversation in which *customers and prospects actually open up to you.*

The VOC Research Process

We conducted 75 interviews for MSC. Rich and his team were actively involved throughout the process by listening to the interviews and working with us to tweak the Interview Guide based on what we learned from the interviews. The organic nature of this VOC process helps generate the maximum amount of value from the interviews.

Rich recalled: "We continued to tweak the questions as we went along—in effect, treating our customers as partners in the VOC process. We tried to get as many people as possible at MSC involved in listening to the interviews. Many people in our company were taken aback by the depth and scope of the responses we received from customers. Once again, involving others in the process along the way helped us to drive acceptance of the results and strategies coming out of the project. It also gave us additional perspectives on what the customers were saying. That's extremely important because this is a qualitative process and open to interpretation."

The VOC Research Findings

Rich summarized the findings from the research as follows:

"We began this process because we wanted to learn more about the impact of the economy on this particular segment of customers. Specifically, we wanted to validate that nothing was 'broken' in our servicing of these customers. What we learned was that the economic downturn had in fact caused a rather drastic change in purchasing behavior.

"While this change seemed to manifest itself as customer attrition, the research learnings revealed that what we were seeing was instead a change in *order frequency*. In other words, we weren't *losing* significant numbers of customers in this sector as a result of the recession; we were witnessing a shift in buying behavior. That was an important, and I might even say critical, piece of market intelligence. It made us question whether we were seeing the beginning of long-lasting changes in the market and whether customers would go back to purchasing patterns seen prior to the recession. Both are yet to be answered, but the knowledge has driven change in how we look at purchasing patterns and which pieces of the MSC value proposition we can emphasize.

"The research revealed that even customers without recent purchases still considered MSC to be an important supplier, and in some cases the primary supplier. And even though we initially looked at the VOC process as a way to figure out what was going on within this particular customer segment, it yielded many broader and unexpected benefits: the research helped to validate the value and services MSC brings to the market and also yielded some significant opportunities to further drive incremental sales within this customer segment. None of these opportunities identified require significant rework of existing services but rather a change in approach to how we communicate MSC services so they are more relevant to our customers.

"There are two examples I can provide to help clarify what we're talking about here. MSC has long marketed our ability to take an order and ship it within the same day. For many years, we have backed this service with a $50 guarantee. More recently, we have enhanced our delivery service to provide next-day delivery throughout the United States. While we marketed this new enhancement, we continued to tout same-day shipping on our marketing vehicles. What the VOC research taught us is that same-day shipping is considered the norm and that next-day delivery is now the minimal accepted level of service. A service we provide but were not marketing strongly enough. The other example has to do with a customer that was looking for a particular inventory management solution. MSC had exactly the solution described, but due to how we were servicing this customer, he had no knowledge of it. As a result, the customer went with another supplier. In both examples, the services exist and require no enhancement. The opportunity lies in how we communicate and market to our customers."

KEY VOC PROCESS LESSON FROM MSC

Use the VOC process to validate (or disprove) key assumptions that could require major investments. In particular, use VOC research to identify the reasons behind unexplained changes in consumer behavior.

In summary, the VOC research delivered the following important benefits for MSC:

- It kept the company from investing time and resources in a campaign to "win back" customers who had not really left at all, but instead had changed their buying patterns.

- It identified competitively powerful strategies for strengthening relationships with customers by adding extra levels of value and benefits that would clearly drive incremental sales.
- It proved that prevailing company assumptions about the necessity to improve or build out certain communication channels with the segment were off base, which meant that the resources that would have been devoted to making these (unnecessary) fixes could be allocated to other projects.
- It validated that the company's existing value proposition and services fit the segment and just needed to be communicated in a manner relevant to the customer.

NOW WHAT?

- Carefully define right objectives for VOC Relationship Research. They should address one or more of these four strategic marketing imperatives:
  - Attracting prospects
  - Converting prospects to customers
  - Selling more to existing customers through better levels of engagement and value
  - Keeping the customers you've got
- Use your customers' in-depth qualitative insights to help validate or question your other business data. Qualitative and quantitative data can tell you what happened yesterday and provide an indication of what *might* happen tomorrow.
- Get as many parts of the organization involved in the VOC project as possible. Get multiple players involved in developing an Interview Guide that will drive the discussion.
- Use the questions your team develops as a starting point, not an ending point. Encourage the customers and prospects you're interviewing to expand on their answers. The value of listening to in-depth conversations with your customers cannot be underestimated. Whatever the original intent of the project, you will find that good VOC research based on these

kinds of conversations can bring value to areas well outside of marketing.

- Look at VOC research as more than a one-off project. In MSC's case, management has gone back to the VOC report and interviews many times, and the VOC has provided the groundwork for other important strategy initiatives. Not surprisingly, the company has made an ongoing commitment to VOC research.

In the next chapter, you'll learn more about the VOC process, the results it has achieved for marketers in other industries, and how you can use it to address your marketing requirements.

CHAPTER 2

USE VOC RELATIONSHIP RESEARCH IN YOUR OWN COMPANY TO DEEPEN CUSTOMER ENGAGEMENT

EXECUTIVE SUMMARY

- Additional proof that VOC research drives bottom-line results and can be applied to any industry can be found in the case studies of two companies: Palms Trading and Life Line Screening.
- These three companies used VOC research to develop strategies for acquiring customers and achieving deeper, longer-lasting relationships with existing customers.
- You can use the VOC process in your industry to accomplish the following:
  1. Significantly deepen the level of engagement with your customers
  2. Gain new insights regarding what offers and/or services and messaging are relevant
  3. Understand what actions and/or experiences and messages will ensure significantly higher purchase and engagement rates
  4. Identify gaps between the brand expectation and the reality of the purchase and service experience

Now that you have some familiarity with the "moving parts" of a VOC research program, let's look at three additional real-world examples of companies that made extraordinary market gains by listening to the Voice of the Customer. Bear in mind that these are only three of hundreds of successful implementations of the VOC process across virtually all industries. As you read, think about how you could use the VOC process to help you address similar challenges you are facing at your company.

CASE STUDY:
TRANSFORMING THE CUSTOMER RELATIONSHIP—
PALMS TRADING

CLOSE-UP ON PALMS TRADING COMPANY
- Founded around 1919
- Offers a huge inventory of Pueblo Pottery and Native American jewelry
- Its 5,000-square-foot showroom in Albuquerque, New Mexico, displays thousands of pieces of Pueblo Pottery, even more Native American jewelry, and hundreds of Navajo rugs, Hopi and Navajo kachinas, and similar Native American handmade artwork.
- www.palmstrading.com

Some of the most beautiful Native American handcrafted artwork can be found at the Palms Trading Company, one of the most successful wholesale and retail purveyors of Native American arts and crafts. A family-owned business, Palms has roots in the frontier days of the early 1900s. Over the years, it has established a reputation for providing a large selection of authentic, high-quality collectible Native American pottery, jewelry, kachinas, and hand-woven Navajo rugs.

The core business is serving consumers who visit its Albuquerque store and wholesalers who sell the merchandise from their own stores. Palms also caters to a small but loyal group of collectors of upscale Native American art.

According to Guy Berger, president of the company, "My relatives settled in New Mexico in the 1800s, thanks to the Homestead Act. Our challenge today is to maintain our legacy as a small Native American Trading Post, yet appeal to a new generation of buyers and collectors who need to be educated and engaged, yet have limited time and patience.

"The goal is to get people into a relationship with Palms so they self-profile their interests regarding pottery, jewelry, and rugs and indicate how they want to do business, that is, any combination of brick-and-mortar retail, phone, trade shows, or the Internet. Additionally, we want to maintain our relationships with the multiple generations of consumer buyers, retail shops, collectors, and the Native American artists from whom we buy art.

"By helping us to conduct our VOC Relationship Research program, Ernan helped us implement twenty-first-century marketing practices in ways that supported the development of our 75-year-old business."

The Objectives of the VOC Research

Guy's reasons for conducting the VOC research were to improve average order size, identify ways to establish longer-term relationships with customers, and understand why certain wholesalers were not purchasing from Palms.

Specific VOC objectives were defined as understanding the following:

- How do customers perceive Palms' strengths and weaknesses?
- How can Palms improve customer relationships, and how will this contribute to increased sales?

- What do customers expect from Palms, and how does Palms meet those expectations?
- Why don't certain companies purchase from Palms?
- How can Palms provide ongoing value and relevant communications going forward?
- What are retailers' perceptions of the clarity and integrity of the wholesale prices that Palms charges?

The Research Sample

Based on these objectives, we interviewed eight people from each of the following groups:

- Decision makers at retail outlets currently buying from Palms
- Prospects from retail outlets not yet buying from Palms
- "Resistors" from retail outlets that weren't engaging with Palms

The Questions

The Interview Guide that emerged from the objectives included the following questions.

ERNAN ROMAN DIRECT MARKETING

1. How important are Native American arts and crafts to your product line?
2. For Native American arts and crafts, how many suppliers do you order from?
3. What are your criteria for choosing a supplier of Native American arts and crafts?
4. Are you staying with your current Native American arts and crafts suppliers, or do you periodically consider changing or adding others? Why?

5. What might cause you to change suppliers or add a new one?
6. What would you say are the strengths of Palms Trading?
7. And what would you say are the weaknesses of Palms Trading?
8. What can Palms Trading do to provide you with exceptional service and value?
9. Have you purchased from the Palms Trading Web site?
10. How satisfied were you with your experiences using the Palms Trading Web site?
11. What would make purchasing on the Web site an even better experience?
12. Have you purchased by calling Palms Trading?
13. How satisfied were you with your experiences when you called to order?
14. What would make purchasing by phone from Palms Trading an even better experience?
15. How satisfied were you with your experiences when you purchased at our store?
16. What would make purchasing at our store an even better experience?

The Takeaways

Perhaps the most surprising outcome of the VOC research we conducted for Palms was the one that uprooted a core assumption of Guy's: the idea that certain wholesalers were predisposed against buying from Palms. This turned out not to be the case.

As one respondent put it, she would be happy to place an order "if Palms called regarding my inventory of XYZ, asked what I needed, how could they help. I would also want someone I could e-mail with a question and a contact who knows my range of products, develops a rapport, and understands my style needs. That person must be patient and must get it right!"

Responses like this indicated that so-called resistors would be willing to do business with Palms, given their impeccable reputation, if only Palms would *proactively reach out to them*. Repeatedly, interviews told us that knowledgeable, caring, honest customer service was an important competitive differentiator—far more important than Palms's pricing, which respondents found fair. *What people wanted was a better connection with the company, via face-to-face, online, and telephone interactions.*

As a result, Palms expanded its Personal Shopper customer service program, which it had developed for its retail clients, and it tailored the program for this wholesale group.

"Following the lead of what we learned in the VOC research," Guy said, "we created a more advanced Personal Shopper program for our wholesale clients to make them feel comfortable and enrich their 'Palms Experience.' Additionally, each of our wholesale clients was assigned a Personal Shopper, or, as one interviewee put it, 'a go-to person' with whom the client could work closely to identify his or her specific price ranges, Pueblo, style, and other preferences. Personal Shopper is our proactive customer service program that educates customers, probes to identify their interests, and enables us to search for their special items in the store, on the Internet or in the Native American Pueblos. Upon finding the item, they are immediately contacted by their Personal Shopper. Our goal is to give our clients the most complete, informative, and pleasant experience we can. This is the difference between our Personal Shoppers and what most people think of when they hear the words 'customer service rep.' Moreover, our program is especially valuable in this industry due to the unique and sometimes very rare nature of the products requested."

In addition, it was critical to expand the Palms opt-in database. (You'll be learning more about opt-in initiatives in the next chapter.) The expanded opt-in program consisted of various channels:

- An in-store Personal Shopper Opt-In form, which Personal Shoppers were trained to ask each customer to complete
- An electronic form on the Palms Web site that included the Personal Shopper Opt-In form
- The *Indian Art Update* e-newsletters that customers could opt in to receive, and updates regarding new inventory that customers could also opt in to receive by e-mail or Personal Shopper calls
- Personal invitations from Personal Shoppers to their respective customers

According to Guy, "'Personal Shopper' is not just a term we use to describe someone's job; it's the way we do business now. This new level of service is incorporated into all of our communications and personnel training. Our Personal Shoppers are continually retrained regarding how to provide our clients with value-added information. Our staff is taught how to find pertinent information on artists—their work and their specific lineage. Items that are not currently in stock, unusual requests, and hard-to-find pieces are also a specialty of the Personal Shopper. Our goal is personalized and informative inbound and outbound customer service that benefits both our customers and Palms. This is a clear and easily distinguishable difference between a 'customer service rep' and our Personal Shoppers."

The VOC initiative also helped Palms to create several Internet strategy initiatives (www.palmstrading.com) to enrich the online experience:

- Provide rich information that puts the art objects in context— from artist biographies to lists of dates and times for Native American feast days and dances.
- Keep a large amount of inventory visible, and update it frequently because these items are handmade and of limited availability.
- Guarantee that the merchandise we sell is authentic.
- Continue to upgrade the site to improve ease of use and navigation.
- Make sure the site is safe and secure for customers by displaying the "security lock" icon, which is backed up by our security certification. This is especially important given the constant concern of fraud in the Native American arts industry.

The Results

Guy's original goal had been to grow bottom-line sales by 5 percent year to year. The actual results in the 12 months following the VOC program were considerably more robust:

- Sales increased 10 percent year to year.
- The opt-in database grew 470 percent over original projections.

According to Guy, "I credit the increase in sales to the power of the VOC research and the Personal Shopper program it helped to improve. This program pushed us to be proactive in caring for and servicing prospects and customers through all of our channels. I also learned a valuable lesson in how much our customers wanted to hear from us, as long as it was relevant and provided benefit to them."

KEY VOC PROCESS LESSON FROM PALMS

Use the VOC research to generate an in-depth understanding of the value customers expect from you. Even if you are a small company and think you are "customer centric," you will be surprised by how much you can learn. The actions you can implement from the VOC will go straight to the bottom line.

One of the most important key performance indicators for any company is the ability to generate strong repeat purchases. Dramatic increases in repeat purchases as a result of implementing learnings from VOC research are common.

CASE STUDY:
MEASURING THE CUSTOMER EXPERIENCE
AND MEASURING CUSTOMER RETENTION—
LIFE LINE SCREENING

CLOSE-UP ON LIFE LINE SCREENING
- Founded in 1993
- The leading provider of community-based preventive health services
- Has screened over 6 million people
- www.lifelinescreening.com

Life Line Screening, like many companies in this book, already had a satisfaction metric in place. In their case, it was called the *net promoter score* (NPS), which you'll learn about in a moment. While valuable, NPS was not designed to generate the in-depth information needed by management to develop strategies for deeper relationship marketing engagement. As Eric Greenberg, vice president marketing, explained, Life Line used VOC research to gain that deeper level of customer insight.

VOC-ABULARY

An organization's *net promoter score* (NPS)—a metric made popular in Fred Reichheld's book *The Ultimate Question*—measures how the average customer responds, on a scale of 1 to 10, to the question, "How likely is it that you would recommend our company to a friend or colleague?"

C O M P A N Y   B R I E F I N G
LIFE LINE SCREENING
ERIC GREENBERG, Vice President of Marketing, Life Line Screening

Life Line Screening provides preventive screenings for approximately 1 million people a year in over 17,000 locations to help customers determine their risk of disease. The painless, noninvasive, and affordable screenings can literally "see" inside your arteries to look for the plaque buildup (atherosclerosis) that causes most heart attacks and strokes; our blood tests look for common markers of disease such as elevated cholesterol and glucose. We help our customers determine their risks early—before they have symptoms—so that they can proactively work with their doctor to prevent an early death or major disability.

Since these kinds of preventive health screenings are not generally paid for by private insurance or Medicare, our customers must pay directly and out of pocket for our discretionary services. This means that consumers are free to purchase from us or a competitor or not at all. So, unlike some health providers, for us customer service means everything. If our customers are not fully satisfied that we have provided value for the money spent, they are under no obligation to return.

Life Line Screening has always been a data-driven company. We measure everything—response rates, call volumes, costs per labor hour, drive times, turnover rates, clinical accuracy, and hundreds of additional data points that help us determine whether we are delivering our service efficiently, accurately, and promptly. And while we have always been customer focused, in early 2009 we decided as a company that we needed to do even more to put the customer first.

We were searching for a way to increase our understanding of our customer satisfaction—and ultimately, customer retention. We knew that what we had been doing was adequate, but we weren't convinced it was superior. I think the turning point for us came when some people on our management team read Fred Reichheld's book *The Ultimate Question*. Reichheld discusses the importance of understanding a company's "net promoter score," or NPS. Companies obtain their net promoter score by asking customers a single question on a 0-to-10 rating scale: "How likely is it that you would recommend our company to a friend or colleague?"

We had been measuring the net promoter score since 2005, but only after reading the book did we start to recognize its importance in improving customer retention. The NPS question is included in our customer feedback survey that we e-mail to customers the day after they are screened. Thousands of customers complete the survey each month and contribute to our monthly NPS score.

In June 2009, we kicked off our Customer First initiative. As part of that initiative, the company "adopted" five of the lowest-scoring NPS teams around the country to see if a concentrated effort could move the needle in a positive direction. Significant effort was placed on listening to customer feedback—positive and negative. A weekly reporting tool for our general managers and the adopted teams allowed them to review team-specific customer comments and scores on a real-time basis. Listening to customer feedback led to recognition of common themes of customer satisfaction and dissatisfaction. We then delivered training blasts to team members regarding key Customer First concepts, which included being friendly, greeting customers, and minimizing wait times.

We then launched the 14-Point Customer Promise Program that was designed to set a high bar of expectations for our providing services to our customers and to remind our employees to put the customers first in all the things they do. We also made an effort to empower our frontline employees to handle common customer complaints and/or issues on the spot, rather than delaying resolution by having to seek permission from a supervisor.

After several months, we started to see a cultural shift within the company and among the adopted teams. Net promoter scores for the teams were rising, and adopted team protocols were rolled out across the rest of the company. As a result, net promoter scores for the latter part of 2009 and early 2010 have reached nearly 70 percent—world class by any standard.

More recently, we have recognized the need for *deeper engagement* with our customers. To help us understand their expectations for higher value relationships, we asked Ernan Roman's firm to conduct in-depth Voice-of-the-Customer research.

The Takeaways

The VOC research has reinforced our interpretation of the NPS data we were seeing, but it has also given us a much deeper qualitative level of understanding of what drives customer behavior.

In Life Line Screening's case, our customers are actually quite satisfied with the service we provide and the value for the money (hence the high NPSs). Yet, sometimes customer satisfaction is not enough. Or, said differently, your customers can be quite satisfied with your product or service but view their experience with you as a worthwhile single event, not the beginning of an *ongoing relationship*.

What we are learning is that our customers trust us and value what we provide them—but they are looking for a *deeper and ongoing engagement*. This means that they are looking for us to be more proactive across all the customer touch points. If we want customers to truly value us as a part of their health-care team, we have to give them more—and often. Whether that means an outbound call to allay their fears before their first screening, or a call to ask them if they understood their screening results—they want more from us. They are looking for us to help provide them information, solutions, and ideas that can help them stay healthy and independent.

NOW WHAT?

As you consider the potential of the VOC Research Process to increase sales or repeat purchases in your own organization, think about using the VOC research to accomplish the following:

- Generate an in-depth understanding of the value customers expect from your company—throughout the major points in their life cycle of experience with your company.
- Identify gaps between the customers' brand expectations and their actual experience with your organization.
- Understand how to establish and maintain relevance across your multiple channels and points of contact.
- Determine the effectiveness of your media mix: Are customers getting too many communications, and with not enough relevance?
- Identify how you can better personalize the customer experience, whether online, in person, or over the phone.

In the next part of the book, you'll learn about the critical principle of *VOC-driven opt-in* and how that differs from what most people think of when they think of opt-in marketing.

CREATE VOC-DRIVEN OPT-IN RELATIONSHIP STRATEGIES

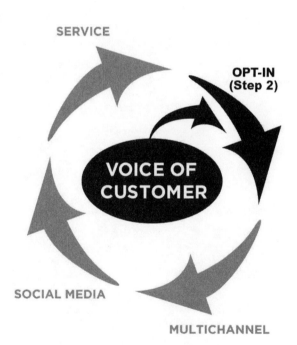

3

OPT-IN RELATIONSHIP STRATEGIES

EXECUTIVE SUMMARY

- True opt-in is about the relationship, not the first contact or first sale.
- An effective Opt-In/Self-Profiling Relationship Strategy begins the process of long-term engagement with the prospect or customer.
- Microsoft's online Business Resource Center is a best-in-class example of the VOC-driven opt-in relationship strategy.
- Simply firing off a few dozen self-profiling opt-in questions is not going to create a relationship. We must "earn the right": explain what information we're asking for, why we're asking for it, and how what we're planning to do with it benefits the other person.

A sad misconception drives many marketing campaigns. It revolves around the much-misunderstood term *opt-in*. What does it really mean?

A FAMILIAR STORY

Let's assume that you work for a company called HugeCo and that you are my target customer. Assume too that, after seeing a news report about your company, you happen to take a look at my Web site (WidgetCo) and spot an article whose title is powerful and compelling enough to make you want to download it: "Fifteen Ways to Reduce Widget Reconditioning Expenses within the Next 30 Days."

As it happens, your CEO has been chewing you out recently about how much you're spending to recondition widgets; the article topic is intriguing, so you click on the link.

Before you can read or download anything, however, you're greeted by a little pop-up box, which reads as follows:

> Thank you for requesting an article from the WidgetCo archive. In order to serve you better, and speed the content that you have requested, we ask that you take just a moment to give us a little more information about yourself and your organization.

There follow no less than 14 boxes for you to fill out, 6 of which are "mandatory" in order to receive the article and 8 of which are "optional."

The six mandatory pieces of information you must provide—at least, if you want to get a glimpse of the content you want—are your full name, your e-mail address, the organization you work for, your job title, company address, city, state, and ZIP code, and the amount of money you spend on widget reconditioning each year. The eight "optional" boxes don't actually come out and ask how much you weigh, what prescription medications your doctor has suggested that you take over the last three years, and whether you've ever inhaled, but for a moment you wonder if they're about to. What is your business phone number? What is your cell phone number? How many years have you been at your present job? What levels of widget purchasing are you personally authorized to make? And so on.

Muttering some choice words to yourself about how long this is taking, you enter all the mandatory information, skip all the optional boxes, and download the article so you can read it, print it, and show it to your CEO.

At that stage, you have not really "opted in" to anything—except a list of people who are authorized to receive the article. You certainly haven't opted in to a meaningful relationship with my organization.

You like the article a lot, but what you don't like quite as much is the tide of e-mail from the WidgetCo marketing department that now clutters your in-box. Over the next 60 days, you receive no less than 26 e-mail messages from them. Of those 26 messages, you open the first 3. All 3 are completely irrelevant to your needs.

Each message comes with a request for "feedback" about what you'd like to see in future mailings. Each gives you the opportunity to stop receiving messages. You're a busy person, so you ignore both that request for feedback . . . and the opportunity to opt out.

What WidgetCo has done to you is not "opt-in marketing" because true opt-in is the process of *actively choosing to enter into a relationship*, not the process of making initial contact.

The WidgetCo's communication is an example of *customer relationship manipulation*. In order to get the free information, you've had to "pay" for it—with your personal information. Having seen so little of value, you will only pay for that information grudgingly, and not with any sense of investment in an ongoing relationship.

Opt-in is *not* about passively agreeing to receive e-mail.

It's about *actively opting in to a relationship* and self-profiling your preferences and aversions as part of your engagement in that relationship.

The fact that so many companies, in so many different industries, follow the "customer relationship manipulation" scenario I have just described, and then use the phrase "opt-in marketing" to describe what they have done, is proof of a disturbing, and widespread, failure to engage in a meaningful way with customers.

I say "failure" for this reason: If I were to call you, 60 days after you had downloaded the article, and ask whether you had ever "opted in" to anything that WidgetCo had to offer, one of two things would probably happen: you would either forget having filled out the form so you could receive the article in the first place, or you would be reminded that you needed to make a request to be dropped from the mailing list!

There is a better way, and it begins with our own willingness to redefine what we mean by "opt in" and in so doing, fundamentally change how we treat our customers and prospects. This chapter will show you how to use true opt-in—that is, an Opt-In/Self-Profiling Relationship Strategy—to begin that essential process of engagement.

CHANGING THE DEFINITION, CHANGING THE PARADIGM

As twenty-first-century marketers, we have a mandate to focus on our *relationships* with prospects and customers. Given the empowerment of decision makers thanks to the Internet and social media, bombarding them with irrelevant marketing information doesn't work. It generates poor response rates, it damages our brand, and it proves that we place no value in that relationship.

In a survey of marketers conducted by Ernan Roman Direct Marketing and the Direct Marketing Association, 35 percent of respondents defined *opt-in marketing* as a customer's or prospect's simply agreeing to receive e-mail. Another 15 percent described *opt-in marketing* as a second request to receive e-mail. Neither of these definitions meets the standards we need to adopt.

Interestingly, when offered the definition "a dialogue in which the customer or prospect actively defines how he or she wants to engage with us, and via what mix of media," 50 percent of the group was willing to adopt it!

OPT IN OR OPT OUT?

What most marketers call "opt-in marketing" is really best understood as "opt-out marketing." Consider these sobering realities of the twenty-first-century marketing landscape, as defined by the consumers who have taken the leading role in shaping it:

- More than 76 percent of U.S. adults have registered for the National Do Not Call (DNC) Registry (Harris Interactive). This amounts to the largest grassroots movement in American history!
- Over 191 million phone numbers are listed in the DNC Registry (source: Federal Trade Commission, Biennial Report to Congress, December 2009).
- Federal antispam legislation (CAN-SPAM) now mandates severe penalties for misleading or unauthorized e-mail marketing campaigns.
- Scores of states have upped the ante by introducing do-not-mail bills.

The National Do Not Call Registry is a database of numbers that has been maintained by the Federal Trade Commission since 2004. It was created in response to overwhelming political pressure from consumers who were sick and tired of getting annoying and irrelevant calls from people with whom they had no existing relationships.

> Federal law provides for a fine of $11,000 for every violation of the law prohibiting calls to consumers listed in the National Do Not Call Registry.

This movement is by no means limited to the United States. The Italian government banned all unsolicited mail, phone, e-mail, fax, and mobile communications sent without *affirmative consent* from the recipient.

Denmark, for its part, has the oldest marketing communications legislation in the world, strictly regulating the ways in which businesses may and may not approach consumers. The Danish law dates back to 1912, and it has been refined and updated several times since then. It has contained all the major elements of the Italian law for more than 40 years. In other words, the consumers in the United States have finally started demanding what consumers in other parts of the world have been demanding for decades.

> Denmark's consumer protection legislation has forced marketers to take a more socially responsible approach than many other marketers take. They *must* think differently than marketers in the United States—if they wish to survive. This process of rethinking the relationship with the customer is now happening around the world. I see this global trend toward greater consumer protection from unsolicited marketing messages as unstoppable. I also see it as inherently positive for the marketing community. The strict guidelines within which all Danish marketers must work might very well be one of the reasons why we see so many Danish direct marketing campaigns winning industry awards, year after year.
>
> —Ole Stangerup, Chief Relationship Officer, Express A/S

Beyond intense pressures from consumers lies the (hardly coinciden-
tal) fact that traditional spray-and-pray marketing simply isn't working
as well as it used to. These days, it's more common than ever to hear
marketers complain about things like "list fatigue"—the phenomenon
whereby a list that used to respond at, say, 2 percent, now responds at
only one-quarter of 1 percent. Actually, it's not really the list that's
tired. It's the central principle that a list can be flogged endlessly for
short-term gain. *That's* what's tired!

What, marketers are likely to ask, is the alternative? The answer is
both simple and direct: an Opt-In/Self-Profiling Relationship Strategy.
This is marketing that engages customers to *define their unique
requirements in response to meaningful value propositions presented by
the marketer.*

As a result of this dialogue, customers populate the enterprise's
opt-in database with uniquely detailed, actionable information. That
database then becomes an *irreplaceable, strategically essential competitive tool.*

As you know, an organization's database is its most important single
asset when it comes to direct marketing. Think of the power and accuracy you would enjoy with a database that contained unique, self-profiled information from beginning to end, information that *you had* and
your competitors didn't.

The marketing organization wise enough to take the steps necessary
to compile that list—and respect the expressed desires of the prospects
and customers who created it—will survive and thrive in the marketplace. The marketing organization that ignores opportunities to create
this kind of dialogue will stagnate, or even perish.

Beyond "Permission"

I hope it's clear now that there is a world of difference between the
kind of discussion I am advocating here and what is commonly understood as "permission-based marketing." For most of today's marketers, permission-based marketing simply means getting someone to
agree to accept an e-newsletter. That's an essentially passive relationship, and it's not one that's going to transform your business or your
market.

What we are talking about is getting customers to take an *active role* in defining the relationship—so that we as marketers can understand exactly what value we need to provide to get customers to share their preferences and expectations for the right message, right offer, sent to the right person, at the right time, and via their medium of choice. This information will then form our uniquely powerful, and accurate, opt-in preference database. Like any good relationship, the one that makes that database possible is one that develops over time and requires multiple steps.

OLD REALITY, NEW REALITY

The Old Reality was one in which marketers dictated both the message and the medium—the channel—by which the message was delivered.

The New Reality—the reality with which we all must come to terms, and quickly—is one in which consumers can and do determine both the message *and* the medium by which that message is transmitted. Today's consumers have realized, after decades of passive acceptance of customer relationship manipulation, that they don't have to allow marketers to dictate the terms of their relationship with us. They can set the agenda and tune in to what they want to, when they want to, and *via the channels of their choice.*

Why Opt-In Is Like Dating

We can compare this multistep engagement to the process of turning a first date into a second date. If someone were to show up on your doorstep for a first date with a long printed list of personal questions—how much do you weigh, whether you like to sleep in on Saturday mornings, how many children you'd like to have—and then open the first discussion with you by reciting that checklist of questions, the likelihood of that person getting a second date would be fairly low.

The same goes for our prospects and customers. They must understand, and feel comfortable with, the many and varied reasons it makes sense to consider deepening and extending the relationship, and they must feel that they are part of the process that determines whether and how that relationship moves forward.

An opt-in relationship strategy allows you to respond to the unique requirements of your customers by gaining an understanding of their relationship requirements *as individuals.* What's remarkable (as the next case study proves) is that you don't need a huge sample of prospects and customers to generate a deep understanding of how your customers respond, on an individual level, to your organization's value propositions. As we saw in Chapters 2 and 3, you can gain incredible insights about what will (and won't) motivate prospects and customers to opt in to your organization by conducting in-depth VOC interviews with a limited sample size.

After you conduct in-depth discussions with a carefully selected sample of prospects and customers about their ideal relationship with your organization, you will be able to accomplish the following:

- Accurately define individual preferences and requirements of a much larger group of prospects and customers
- Learn exactly what prospects and customers expect of you in the framework of an opt-in relationship
- Learn how to leverage the dimension of time to sustain the value and/or relevance you provide
- Populate your organization's opt-in database with self-profiled preferences

The opt-in/self-profiling process requires the following:

- A fundamental rethinking of how you value a customer relationship
- A change in business metrics and compensation to focus on long-term Customer Lifetime Value (CLTV) and long-term customer satisfaction as key performance indicators
- Operational precision in managing offers and communications per individual customer requirements
- Commitment in the face of challenge

Make no mistake: This change process can be a challenge to implement, especially in larger organizations. People up and down the line, occupying all levels of the organization must "get it," and they must find a way to make the customers' priorities for the relationship the *organization's* priorities for the relationship.

Think of VOC research as the driving gear in a precision marketing machine. Think of the opt-in/self-profiling process as the next gear, the one that that will drive the messaging and offer process, *per the preferences of customers.*

Here's one of my favorite examples of an organization that "got it." This case study is the perfect "proof-of-concept" for people who ask, "What do you mean by 'opt-in'? How does it connect to the Voice of the Customer, and why is any of this important? What bottom-line results does VOC-driven opt-in generate?"

CASE STUDY:
MICROSOFT BUSINESS RESOURCE CENTER

CLOSE-UP ON MICROSOFT
- Founded in 1975
- Headquarters: Redmond, Washington

- Microsoft (Nasdaq: MSFT) is the worldwide leader in software, services, and solutions that help people and businesses realize their full potential.
- Approximately 93,000 employees
- www.microsoft.com

Microsoft's achievements with its relationship program and in particular one of the core assets, the online Business Resource Center, confirm the enduring value of opt-in. The Business Resource Center engages customers to commit to defining a value-added relationship and what a marketer has to do to earn and sustain the customer's engagement over time. The opt-in marketing strategy in this case study seems so straightforward and so logical—especially when you look at the process that was used to launch Microsoft's special, carefully targeted Business Resource Center. I suspect you will begin to wonder why more companies, why *all* companies, don't engage customers and prospects in this way. Indeed, opt-in is the natural extension of the Voice-of-the-Customer Relationship Research you have been reading about here.

The Situation

Microsoft's product sales within the Small and Midsize Business (SMB) segment, which includes more than 20 million companies, are largely generated through a network of business partners. These partners represent the *main* contact points for SMB firms purchasing Microsoft products. As a result, these millions of small and medium-sized businesses, which range from home-based businesses with a single computer to much larger "midmarket" companies with hundreds of computers, have almost no direct relationship with Microsoft.

We were brought in to work with Microsoft because the company faced a challenge. As Lisa Clawson, senior marketing manager at Microsoft, put it: "Although the customers in this segment had favorable responses to the software they used, there was not an effective relationship with the company that produced and supported these products. To these users, Microsoft was famous as a global brand—but virtually unknown as a business partner. Creating and supporting relationships with customers within this group was a clear priority for us, given the strategic importance of the segment. But the question remained, how should we approach this large, diverse SMB segment?"

After business analyses, it was determined that we needed to provide varying levels of support and resources from high-touch to self-service resources in order to adequately serve this vast market segment. Research indicated that decision makers across the SMB segment were quite comfortable interacting online. The next step was logical: Microsoft would create a special online resource to support the relationship program. This idea quickly gained traction within Microsoft, in part because past Voice-of-the-Customer (VOC) research had indicated that most of these customers would welcome a deeper relationship with Microsoft. "Past research informed us," Lisa Clawson recalled, "that there were specific levers within the post-purchase life cycle that improved customer satisfaction, and we also knew that there were foundational pillars of the relationship program that customers identified that they wanted—*support, relevant communications, community,* and *training.* So, what we wanted to do was to specifically learn more about how we could drive deeper engagement within those pillars."

Microsoft's major questions at this point included:

- Will an online relationship program appeal to businesses with up to 500 employees?
- Will decision makers in the target group opt in to a deeper level of relationship and self-profile their preferences?
- What are the key enhancements that can help deepen customer engagement?

These questions helped us define the following objectives for the VOC Relationship Research that would tell Microsoft how to build an online relationship program to truly engage customers by providing meaningful value—as defined by customers.

Objectives for the VOC Relationship Research

The objectives Microsoft identified were to gain an in-depth understanding of the following:

- How training, support, community, and communication could drive deeper engagement
- What would drive deeper engagement
- How the communication strategy should be improved to deliver greater value, relevance, and engagement
- How to encourage customers to opt in to self-profile their preferences in order to drive targeted communications
- What the customers' perceptions were regarding the use of customers' opt in self-profiled information

Learnings from the VOC Relationship Research

Here are a few of the specific lessons that Microsoft learned from the VOC Relationship Research interviews driven by those objectives.

Learning 1. The value of the relationship program must be obvious and differentiated.

The VOC research revealed that these customers had a fundamental requirement when it came to using an online resource center from Microsoft: *For goodness' sake, make it easy.* If the site offered more complexity to busy decision makers' already complex day, users would see no value in it. If the site wasn't user friendly and was just a scaled-down version of the site Microsoft had already created for large enterprise customers or for general consumers, members of the target audience would see no benefit. They didn't want to spend a lot of time searching for value. They had more than enough confusion in their day already.

Specifically, prospective users in the target group demanded that the online resource center do the following:

- Provide easy, user-friendly site navigation.
- Use clear, easy-to-understand English, with no knowledge of "tech speak" required to complete key word searches.

- Provide simple access to information and business solutions from every part of the site—no unnecessary page hopping.

In addition, prospective users demanded that Microsoft *keep it focused*. They wanted a one-stop, convenient resource that was clearly different from other existing resources. Respondents wanted every facet of their experience on the site to prove that they had invested their (valuable) time, effort, energy, and attention in the right place.

Small and midsized business customers also expected Microsoft to *deliver "wins."* In essence, this meant making initial interactions with the site engaging by offering quick, painless how-to information and pointing users toward industry, business, and technology information they could act on immediately.

Learning 2. Personalize the experience according to specific attributes.

Prospective users of the site did not want to feel as though they were getting recycled information originally created for the enterprise customers Microsoft serves. They urged Microsoft to *focus on—and satisfy—the specific needs of SMB customers*.

They urged that the site be developed from the SMB user's perspective, not from Microsoft's perspective. That meant requesting, and listening to, user feedback at every single touch point. What's more, VOC respondents wanted that feedback to launch a process of providing *relevant* content and communication to the individual user. In other words, the unique information that individual users provided should populate newsletter and e-mail communications that were *obviously relevant* to that specific reader's world. (See Figure 3.1.)

Another key requirement identified by interviewees was that Microsoft *satisfy different needs*. That meant not only targeting content based on what kind of business someone worked for and what product usage history someone had but also targeting content based on the *purpose* a given user had in coming to the site in the first place. The VOC research identified a few very different psychographics for these online customers, where each of these constituencies demanded customized content from Microsoft and had different expectations from the site.

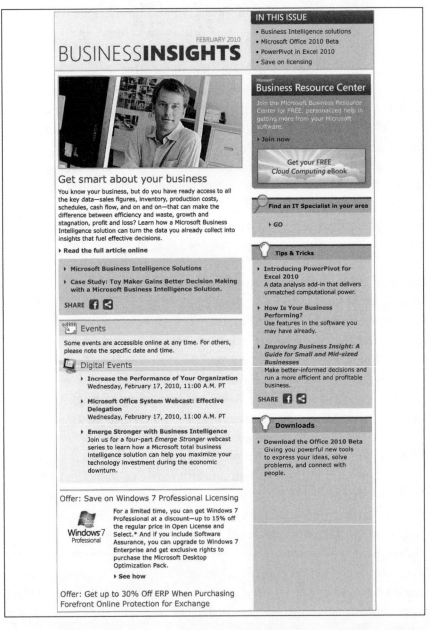

Figure 3.1: VOC research revealed that prospective users of the online resource center demanded customized communications that were obviously relevant to a user's demographics and firmagraphics. The e-newsletter in the figure is an example of customized communication driven by opt-in user information. *Source: Microsoft*

Learning 3. Tie training, support, and community into a *differentiating relationship.*

Based on the learnings from the VOC research, we recommended that training be offered to users as a key benefit early on in the experience and that future training be used to encourage the next level of on-site interaction. We urged Microsoft to offer user-defined training categories for easy access and to make training easy to share. In addition, the VOC research suggested that Microsoft enhance the perceived value of the support it would offer on the site—first and foremost by keeping the site simple and focused (as noted above) but also by leveraging the experience of peers to offer additional support to users. This peer interaction would do much more than solve specific problems. It would lead to a sense of shared community that could be facilitated across a variety of demographic and business areas. In fact, the VOC research defined "three-dimensional" interaction:

> Interaction with peers was the first, most important value point; second was interaction with experts; and third was improved interaction with Microsoft itself. Understanding these three levels of value was essential to creating an engaged community of SMB software users.

A Multitiered Approach

As Lisa Clawson told us, "It became clear from the VOC research that Microsoft should offer separate opt-in opportunities: one for the initial access to the program and other points for subsequent communications. At each stage, Microsoft would need to demonstrate to prospective members the *value* of self-profiling to receive targeted, relevant communications.

"In exchange for the first round of opt-in information, we provided tangible value such as training on a topic of particular interest, selected from a list of popular training programs. In exchange for that value, the user would be more likely to provide the opt-in/self-profiling information."

Following is the initial "wave" of opt-in questions as part of the value exchange with potential users of the relationship resources:

- Name
- E-mail
- Primary role in company (that is, sales, marketing, finance)
- Microsoft software usage and/or ownership
- Number of employees
- Industry
- Primary customer business need
- The biggest challenge facing your organization today
- Number of PCs
- Number of servers

In the future, as the relationship with each individual member deepens, additional questions will be asked as part of this dynamic profiling process. Additional information requests will focus on learning more about the person's business and IT capabilities, interests, and/or needs.

Lisa explained the profiling strategy on this point as follows: "Our goal is to limit the number of questions up front because we have a strategy to build a more comprehensive profile of our customer in order to create a better relationship with that customer as we go along. So rather than asking too many questions about the customer up front, we want to be able to ask mini-sets of questions that are immediately relevant to the actions they take with us."

Lisa's comment serves as ample proof that Microsoft understood the principle of the Value-Exchange Cycle.

The Value-Exchange Cycle

The most important lesson Microsoft learned about opt-in—and indeed the lesson that every marketer who wants to succeed in the current market environment must learn about opt-in—has to do with respect. A special kind of transaction—one rooted in respect and mutual benefit—must take place if we expect prospects and customers to give us detailed information about themselves. In exchange for information about the prospect or customer, we must first *give* something. Specifically, we must *give* evidence of present or future relevancy to something that person is trying to accomplish. Simply firing off a few dozen questions is not going to create a relationship. We must explain what we're asking for, why we're asking for it, and how what we're planning to do with the information we receive relates to the other person's world.

Think of this process as a *value exchange*. The more relevant information we *give* the consumer about why we're asking the person what we're asking, and the clearer we are about what value we will be able to deliver in that person's world as a result of getting that information, the better the quality of the opt-in profile information we will receive in return. If we offer only undifferentiated messaging, we will never begin the process of engagement that makes the Value-Exchange Cycle possible.

THE VALUE-EXCHANGE CYCLE

Relevancy and perceived value in a prospect's or customer's world *drives* better opt-in information, which *drives* greater relevancy and perceived value in the prospect's or customer's world, which *drives* better opt-in information, . . . ad infinitum.

Microsoft Harnesses the Power of the Value-Exchange Cycle

As we rolled out the program, there were tiers of targeted customers for Microsoft's new online Business Resource Center for small and midsized businesses (SMBs). The Business Resource Center site was designed to deliver a clear VOC-driven set of benefits for customers in each tier—with the costliest benefits, from Microsoft's point of view, for customers in the top tier (Figure 3.2).

Throughout the process, specific feedback from small business owners served as Microsoft's "compass point" for the repositioning of the company's relationship with the target market. The VOC research provided Microsoft with customer guidance plus actionable strategies and tactics to help implement a deeper customer engagement.

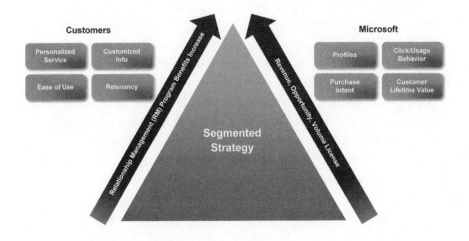

Figure 3.2: VOC-Driven SMB Relationship Program   *Source: Microsoft*

ON THE WEB: THE BUSINESS RESOURCE CENTER
Keep your business moving.

Join the Microsoft Business Resource Center for FREE personalized help to get more from your Microsoft software.

This Value-Exchange Cycle gave customers in the target sector the following:

- Personalized service
- Customized information
- Ease of use
- Relevancy

At the same time, the Value-Exchange Cycle gave Microsoft the following:

- Invaluable opt-in profile information
- Invaluable information on click and usage behavior
- Invaluable information on purchase intent
- Substantial cross-selling opportunities

Unprecedented Results

In implementing this opt-in program and launching the Microsoft Business Resource Center (currently up and running at www.microsoft .com/business/mycenter), the following results have been achieved:

- Opt-in rates range between 45 and 95 percent depending upon the customer tier.
- Open rates have improved by more than 100 percent.
- Response rates are currently performing in the *double digits.*
- Renewal rates are higher with customers in the relationship program.
- Microsoft is receiving very positive customer feedback from the program.

What else is expected?

- *Revenue is expected to continue being greater than the control population.*
- Customers are expected to continue to report significantly greater satisfaction.

As Lisa Clawson observed, "These results are unprecedented."

This is what *true opt-in* can achieve—not just for big organizations like Microsoft but for enterprises of all sizes, as the next chapter will show.

NOW WHAT?

Keep in mind these key takeaways from the Microsoft case study:

- Opt-in is about engaging customers to take an *active role in defining the relationship* so we can understand exactly what value we need to provide to get customers to share their preferences and expectations for the right message, right offer, sent to the right person, at the right time, and via his or her medium of choice. This information will then form our uniquely powerful and accurate opt-in preference database.
- Make sure the value of opting into a relationship with your organization is obvious and differentiated.
- Personalize the experience according to the unique self-profiling information of the customer.
- Find ways to remind the user *how* you are customizing his or her experience.
- Don't promise value during the opt-in process that you can't deliver because the penalty for not delivering once you have raised expectations can be huge.
- *Keep the customer engaged after the initial contact*—otherwise the data you have collected will quickly become irrelevant, and the relationship will die.

In the next chapter, you'll see more examples of how VOC-driven opt-in can deepen and strengthen relationships with customers—and create powerful competitive differentiation.

4

THE SIX PRINCIPLES OF
SUCCESSFUL OPT-IN

EXECUTIVE SUMMARY

- Establishing VOC-driven, opt-in/self-profiling relationships with consumers will improve marketing results and establish a competitive advantage, for any company of any size in any industry.
- When you follow the guidelines outlined in this chapter, your opt-in process will enable you to identify, with great precision, exactly what value, services, and communications your customers want, and don't want, to receive from you.
- The Disney case study will show you how a master marketer ensures the delivery of relevant and targeted communications.

The Microsoft case study makes it clear: you can't serve your customers properly if you don't know what they want. And if you don't know what your existing customers want, how on earth are you going to determine what your prospective customers are likely to want?

If you remember nothing else from this book, remember this: creating VOC-driven, opt-in/self-profiling relationships will establish a major competitive advantage for any company in any industry. The unique database containing the opt-in preferences of your prospects and customers—the specific things that people tell you they want to

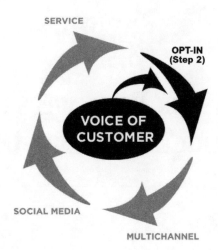

receive, when they want to receive them, and how they want to receive them, as well as what they do not want to receive—should be considered the Holy Grail, your organization's ultimate marketing asset. As you implement the VOC-driven strategies, this asset will become an essential tool for building long-term relationships.

Questions people have after thinking about opt-in for themselves and their enterprises typically include these: Can smaller organizations experience the same kinds of results? How can the opt-in approach be adapted to my industry? What should the opt-in questions sound like? In this chapter, you'll get insights and case studies that answer all of these questions.

DOES OPT-IN WORK FOR SMALLER COMPANIES AS WELL AS LARGER ONES?

Opt-in is definitely not reserved for industry giants like Microsoft. In fact, smaller organizations are usually in a much better position than larger organizations to implement these programs because there are fewer layers of bureaucracy to contend with and thus fewer internal obstacles to launching and implementing the program.

Up-front investments of time and money in creating the opt-in relationship may be quite modest for smaller organizations. What is nonnegotiable, however, regardless of the size of the company, is senior leadership's commitment to making the creation, and ongoing development, of opt-in relationships with customers and prospects an organizational priority—that is, their commitment to making such relationships central elements of "what we do here." Experience has shown that this cultural shift is, as a rule, easier to manage in smaller and midsized organizations than in larger ones.

The size of an organization is not as important as the power of its value proposition for opting in and the credibility of its assurances that the information gathered will be treated with respect. Often, the communications, messages, and offers requested in an opt-in relationship can be delivered with great economy through an automated contact management system. Such a system can deliver relevant content, in accordance with the customer's or prospect's preferences and, just as important, can help suppress information that should not be sent.

Here's the perspective of an online music company, Songza Media, Inc., that uses VOC-driven, opt-in preferences to communicate with its audience:

In the final analysis, the real test of any opt-in program is not the size of the company, but the power and value its opt-in offers. Those offers should be tested in the VOC research to determine how customers and prospects define relevance and value, and to motivate the person to ask "How do I opt in? What do you need to know about me in order for me to get the relevant information you're offering?"

As that discussion with the customer moves forward, it's essential that the person know exactly how his or her personal or business information is going to be used to provide value as he or she has defined it. But that conversation can only take place once you make the right offer.

—Elias Roman, CEO,
Songza Media, Inc.

WHAT KINDS OF OPT-IN QUESTIONS ARE EFFECTIVE AND APPROPRIATE?

Here are some additional examples of the types of questions that have been asked as part of successful opt-in programs. These questions must be presented as part of an overall relationship marketing program that states that as a result of VOC research, the company has learned what customers and prospects expect in a deeper relationship that provides greater value and more relevant communications and services. The message should focus on demonstrating a commitment to provide reciprocal value to the customer or prospect. The reciprocity must clear: you trust us with your detailed business or personal information, and we will use it responsibly to drive relevant and targeted content *as you define it*.

It's important to emphasize that no matter what the content of your questions is, the underlying message must always be the same: *"If you trust us with important information, we will use it to provide increasingly targeted and relevant information, according to your individual needs and preferences."*

Once this message is clearly communicated, you will be surprised by how much sensitive information prospects and customers are willing to share with you. For a health-care marketer, VOC research determined that consumers were willing to share the following information to ensure the receipt of relevant health-care information for themselves and their families:

- Gender
- Age
- Primary risk factors
- Family medical history
- Health-related topics and news of interest
- Specific types of information they would like to receive for family members, that is, spouse, child, or relative

For some technology business-to-business marketers we've worked with, VOC research determined that IT executives would be comfortable providing the following information in exchange for relevant information and offers:

- Contact information
- Specific technology and business topics of interest to them
- Industry
- Job role or function
- Business size and/or number of employees
- Years in business
- Software used
- Software applications
- Level of the IT executives
- Future software needs
- Systems currently being used
- Timetable for upgrades

In the first case, consumers were willing to provide highly sensitive information about their medical history only because they were convinced the information would be treated with respect and confidentiality. Furthermore, they knew that, by sharing this data, they would receive important information that would help them stay healthy.

In the second case, senior IT executives were willing to share confidential information about their company because they knew the information would be treated with respect and confidentiality and that by sharing this information, they would receive important information to help them perform their jobs better.

In each case, the questions were asked only after the marketer had made a high-value offer, pretested in the VOC research, to ensure that the offer would resonate with the respective audiences.

CASE STUDY:
THE DISNEY EXPERIENCE

CLOSE-UP ON THE WALT DISNEY COMPANY
- Founded in 1923
- Headquarters: Burbank, California
- Global entertainment conglomerate whose divisions include the following:

- ○ The Walt Disney Studios
- ○ Disney-ABC Television Group
- ○ ESPN Inc. (majority owner)
- ○ Disney Interactive Media Group
- ○ Disney Consumer Products
- ○ Walt Disney Parks and Resorts
- ○ Marvel Entertainment
- • Over 150,000 employees
- • www.disney.com

In the business-to-consumer realm, one of the most dynamic practitioners of effective opt-in marketing is the Walt Disney organization. We wanted to know how this company, known around the world for its superb branding initiatives, motivated consumers to share information. We were fortunate to discuss Disney's experience-based marketing strategies and compelling value propositions with Scott Hudgins, director of global customer managed relationships for Disney Destinations.

Scott's primary focus is attracting visitors to Disney properties. "Clearly, we take the question of engagement with guests and potential guests very seriously," he said. "We have a responsibility to make sure as many people as possible choose to stay in a dialogue with Disney as a whole."

We asked Scott to identify some of the guiding principles he uses to drive opt-in discussions with potential and current visitors to the Disney parks and resorts. He shared insights about the strategies and tools Disney uses to create and sustain the opt-in discussion—including an innovative personalized map of the theme park, based on preferences expressed online. The map, mailed to prospective guests, transforms the upcoming visit from the world of theoretical possibility to the world of physical reality.

"As far as generating opt-in information goes, one important goal is to make the online exchange of information easy. You don't want to make people go through a lot of detailed registration forms, or make it feel laborious for the guest to have to share information with us. So one example of how we try to make it easy to opt in is our application for customized maps, which we offer through My Disney Vacation, part of our Web site.

For a glimpse at some innovative business-to-consumer opt-in strategies, visit My Disney Vacation online at disneyworld.disney. go.com/wdw/myVacation.

"We have other tools that say, in essence, 'Okay, what attractions are you interested in, or which park do you want to go to first?' But we also have this suite of customized maps that take guests on a different kind of journey and that serve as fun, interactive tools, where they can choose all their favorite characters, their favorite attractions, where they want to go. And we provide them a free keepsake map based on what they've told us. We've actually found that a lot of those guests put the map on their walls as a reminder of the trip they're about to take, as opposed to actually bringing it to the parks with them.

"What that allows us to do is learn a lot about what that guest is interested in. We're obtaining the information in a way that delivers obvious value. This is more effective when it comes to building a relationship than simply giving people a form and saying, 'Hey, what are you interested in?' We're giving them a fun way of engaging with us. You're obtaining a customer's profile, but you're not doing it by throwing questions at the person. You're getting the profile by engaging the person in something that's fun and intuitive and valuable to him or her.

We're obtaining the information in a way that delivers obvious value. This is more effective when it comes to building a relationship than simply giving people a form and saying, "Hey, what are you interested in?"
—SCOTT HUDGINS, DISNEY DESTINATIONS

"Now, the information that we get from that process is incredibly important. For example, just knowing someone's favorite character is a very powerful tool for us in terms of the types of content and the types of experiences people have once they're on site. Knowing that helps us to customize what we need to provide them. So maybe we already know they have young children, but now we know that they're more into the Princess types of experiences; that means we're going to follow up with a series of contacts that emphasize the Princess motif with characters like Cinderella and Ariel before, during, and after the trip.

"We find that the most powerful way to understand who our guests are and what those guests want is to allow them to maintain the profile themselves, in a place where they see value in communicating that profile. And that's what we strive to do at My Disney Vacation online. We find that if you provide immediate, recognizable value to the guests for having shared the information, people will want to engage with you. One example of this is our vacation planning video. There's a clear offer, a clear cause and effect there. People think, 'Okay. I'm going to provide this information, and when I'm done, I'm going to receive a free video.' It all comes down to making sure that we have a very trusted relationship with our guests. And anything that builds up that trust has a positive economic impact on us; by the same token, anything that diminishes that trust has an economic impact on us.

"Another example occurs when people leave the Web site without having booked. If they leave the site but they gave us information while they were there, we'll reestablish contact within 24 hours with what we call a 'shopper' e-mail. This message is not meant to be sales-y; it's just meant to recap everything that happened on the site for them and to give them all the upcoming events that the information connects to. 'Here's the resort you looked at, here are some special events, and here are some fun things to think about for the kids based on the kinds of things you looked at.' As I say, we're very, very careful not to be too sales-y in these communications. Instead, we want to focus most on having the guests have a great experience through every interaction, no matter what that experience is. All the way through the whole relationship, no matter where they are in the process of booking a visit, our goal is to deliver the Disney experience. So the message is not about selling something. It's about being relevant and engaging with people. And if we can hit that standard, then people are going to have a more relevant experience with us while they're online. The future contacts that they see from us are going to be very valuable and relevant based on that engagement, and they're going to want to stay engaged.

"Our business model is based on differentiation through high-quality services and experiences, and so we see every interaction as an opportunity to create a positive experience for our guests. We believe that, if you do that properly, you're going to be blurring the lines between many traditional functions. You're blurring the line between sales and marketing, for instance. Everyone, ultimately, is responsible for some part of the experience, and that means everyone who connects with a guest or prospective guest is approaching that person from a position of service. To do that, you have to have a working knowledge of what part of the experience the person has responded to positively in the past. That's opt-in."

DISNEY OPT-IN MAGIC

The Disney Web site gathers opt-in information by means of games, e-mail updates, and customized create-a-map tools. Here's the Web offering for that personalized map. Notice that it offers value before it asks for information.

Customized Maps

Get FREE, full-color, keepsake-quality Customized Park Maps delivered right to your home, or print them out at any time.

Great vacation planner: Highlight your family's favorite Park activities, and explore all that the Parks have to offer.

Fun and easy: Select your favorites using our fun, easy-to-use interactive Park Maps. You can automatically add the top 10 attractions and entertainment favorites for each Park, chosen with your family in mind.

Free delivery to your home: Order your free Customized Maps, and have them delivered to your home in two to four weeks once every six months.

Choose a theme: Select a cool border theme for each Map.

Source: Disney

Similarly, Disney's online Create-a-Fairy game gives parents and children (typically moms and daughters) an incentive to share information about character preferences. Before I began working on this chapter, a friend mentioned that his wife and daughter had created a new fairy with this high-quality game, and they were happy to supply ample information to Disney in doing so.

About Pixie Hollow

Experience the wonder and magic of Tinker Bell's world when you create your very own Fairy and take flight into Pixie Hollow for high-flying fun and endless excitement! Parents can join in with our Arrival Day Kit.

To see for yourself how Disney leverages these kinds of family-centered online games to create a dialogue that successfully elicits opt-in information from prospective guests and customers, visit disney.go.com/fairies.

THE SIX PRINCIPLES OF
SUCCESSFUL OPT-IN

The core principles of a good opt-in program are logical and applicable to any industry. These principles have been articulated well and concisely by my industry colleagues Don Peppers and Martha Rogers, Ph.D., of the Peppers & Rogers Group.

GETTING HONEST FEEDBACK
FROM YOUR CUSTOMERS, HONESTLY
Don Peppers and Martha Rogers, Ph.D.

Tapping into feedback from customers is an immensely powerful tactic for improving a company's sales and marketing success. But customers will share information only with companies they trust not to abuse it. Here are some ways to earn this trust:

Use a Flexible Opt-In Policy

Many opt-in policies are all-or-nothing propositions, in which customers must elect either to receive a flood of communications from the firm, or none. A flexible opt-in policy will allow customers to indicate their preferences with regards to communication formats, channels, and even timing. So, to the extent possible, give your customers a choice of how much communication to receive from you, or when, or under what conditions.

Establish a Value Exchange

Customers generally don't mind disclosing information if it results in personalized communications or service. So ask yourself what benefits you can provide a customer when the customer provides you with useful information. Can you make your product more relevant? More timely? Less expensive?

Tread Cautiously with Targeted Web Ads

Even though targeted online ads are popular with marketers, research shows that consumers are especially wary of sharing information when targeted Web ads are the result. We're not saying, "don't do it." All we're saying is, "don't pile on." In any case, for behavioral targeting to succeed, you have to have the customer's informed consent.

Make It Clear and Simple

Have a clear, readable privacy policy for your customers to review. Procter & Gamble provides a splendid example. Instead of posting a lengthy document written in legalese, P&G presents a one-page, easy-to-understand set of highlights outlining the policy, with links to more detailed information. By contrast, Sears Holding Company, in its online offer to consumers to join the "My Sears Holding Community," has a scroll box outlining the privacy policy that holds just 10 lines of text and requires 54 boxfuls just to get through the whole policy. Buried far into the policy is a provision that lets the firm install software on your computer that "monitors all of the Internet behavior that occurs on the computer. . . ."

Create a Culture of Customer Trust

Emphasize the importance of privacy protection to everyone who handles personally identifiable customer information, from the CEO to contact center workers. Line employees provide the customer experiences that matter, and employees determine whether your privacy policy becomes business practice or just a piece of paper. If your business culture is built around acting in the interest of customers at all times, then it will be second nature at your company to protect customers from irritating or superfluous uses of their personal information—things most consumers will regard as privacy breaches, whether they formally "agreed" to the data use or not.

Remember: You're Responsible for Your Partners Too

It should go without saying that whatever privacy protection you promise your customers, it has to be something your own sales and channel partners—as well as your suppliers and other vendors—have also agreed to, contractually. Anyone in your "ecosystem" who might handle your own customers' personally identifiable information and feedback will have the capacity to ruin your own reputation. So take care not to let that happen!

Note: Don Peppers and Martha Rogers, Ph.D., are founding partners at the Peppers & Rogers Group. Their most recent book is
*Rules to Break & Laws to Follow: How Your Business Can Beat
the Crisis of Short-Termism* (Wiley, 2008).

When you follow the guidelines outlined above, your opt-in process
will enable you to identify, with great precision, exactly what information and offers your customers want, when, and via what mix of media.

NOW WHAT?

Make sure your opt-in program adheres to these six principles
outlined above:

- Use a flexible opt-in policy.
- Make it clear and simple.
- Establish a value exchange.
- Tread cautiously with targeted Web ads.
- Create a culture of customer trust.
- Remember: You're responsible for your partners too.

In the next part of the book, you'll learn how to take the opt-in preference information and use it to create a multichannel strategy that
leverages the strengths of key elements of the media mix and deploy
them in accordance with the individual preferences of your customers.

CREATE A VOC-DRIVEN MULTICHANNEL MIX

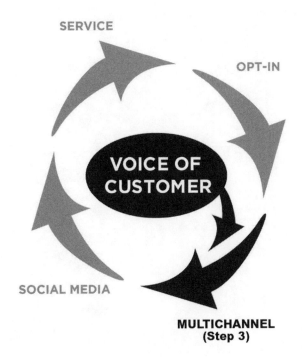

SERVICE

OPT-IN

VOICE OF CUSTOMER

SOCIAL MEDIA

MULTICHANNEL
(Step 3)

5

LEVERAGING THE POWER OF A PREFERENCE-DRIVEN MULTICHANNEL MIX

EXECUTIVE SUMMARY

- Today's empowered consumers are demanding dramatic changes in their relationships with marketers.
- These consumers live in a multichannel world; many of the channels they choose are interactive.
- Aligning your organization's channel strategies with the preferences of your prospects and customers is one essential response to that change.
- So is synchronizing your message across channels.
- Today's consumers expect to be heard. The marketers who are willing to listen to them will establish a significant competitive edge.

Customer service is emphatically a marketing channel. That point, covered in depth later in this book, is worth mentioning as we begin our discussion of multichannel initiatives. Why? Because these days, customers have channels of their own to bring into play when they don't like what they experience in the customer service channel!

Case in point: in 2010, a Minnesota moviegoer wrote a complaint e-mail to the owners of a local multiplex about the poor service she had received during a recent night out. She took the theater to task for not taking debit or credit cards, for letting the ATM in the lobby run out of cash, and for interrupting the evening's entertainment by sending ushers with flashlights into the cinema to check people's tickets. "I did not pay $18 to have a distracted experience," her e-mail explained. "I would rather drive to White Bear Lake, where they obviously know how to run a theater, than have this experience again."

The following morning she got this reply from a vice president of the chain that owned the cinema. "Drive to White Bear Lake and also go [expletive] yourself," it read. "If you don't have money for entertainment, get a better job, and don't pay for everything on your credit or check card."

Only a few years ago, that intemperate reply to a customer complaint would have earned the VP a private reprimand—or perhaps have been ignored entirely. In the era in which we now live, however, that hastily typed, hastily sent message was enough to create a public relations disaster of unimaginable proportions for the owners of the multiplex. The offended moviegoer posted the VP's crass response on her Facebook page. Within 72 hours, a host of outraged readers—over 3,300 of them—had joined a grassroots campaign to boycott the cinema. A tidal wave of bad press followed.

Yes. File the episode under "Don't let this happen to you." But don't stop there. Join the revolution!

THE GAME CHANGE

A "game change" has already taken place—not just in Minnesota but in all critical sectors of the global economy. This change has had, and will continue to have, a profound effect on all marketers. As do so many other changes, this change challenges us to leave behind the comforting, but irrelevant, realities of years past. This game change is one that grants comparatively more authority in the relationship to consumers, and comparatively less to marketers. This change has confirmed what many of us have long suspected: that *consumers,* not marketers, are the center of the marketing universe.

We no longer live in a world where consumers will put up with mistreatment silently, suffer through unsolicited marketing calls at the dinner hour, or ignore an inbox stuffed with unwanted e-mail. Marketers who believe their business plans can survive a pattern of abusive, undifferentiated, or just plain ill-conceived communications with consumers remind me a little bit of the authorities who interrogated the scientist Galileo in the 1600s. Those "authorities" of over four centuries ago clung stubbornly to that which had become familiar to them. No matter how insistent the guardians of the status quo were about getting Galileo to swear that the sun revolved around earth, the sun nevertheless remained the center of the solar system. There's a lesson there for marketers: sometimes, our own preconceptions blind us to the realities of the universe in which we live.

Our advertising, our frontline service providers, our complaint-response mechanisms, our social media presence—these and many more points of contact represent the *channels* through which we communicate with customers. How well we integrate and deploy these tools, as the owners of that Minnesota multiplex quickly learned, is sometimes open to question.

THE FACTS OF THE MATTER

Whether we like it or not, whether we choose to acknowledge it or not, whether it adheres to what we were taught in marketing textbooks or not, the engaged consumer is now, and will always be, the center of our universe.

That means that the channel decisions we make must be driven not by what is familiar or convenient from our point of view as marketers but by the clear preferences expressed by the Voice of the Customer.

Consumers have seized control of the communication process. We have no choice but to engage them in meaningful *conversations*, not bombard them with irrelevant messages using media they have not chosen.

THE LIMITS OF PUSH

"Push marketing"—by which I mean marketing that sees consumers as essentially passive beings until they are stirred to action by messages we cook up in the conference room or the cubicle—is no longer enough.

The push marketing model is based on the principle of "commanding" the consumer to do something. It has been associated with direct mail, radio, television, telephone, and print advertisements for decades. It seeks to change perceptions and behaviors in the marketplace by repeating a sometimes memorable message—often, an undifferentiated message "targeted" to vast subgroups of prospective buyers assumed to have common interests. The effectiveness of push marketing is relatively easy to gauge: we simply measure how often the consumer takes the desired action after exposure to the message.

Push marketing has been very effective for decades. Historically, however, it has always been transaction oriented, not discussion oriented.

> Push marketing has indeed driven countless billions of dollars in sales—but it did so during a time when consumers and technology were very different than they are today.

Today's consumers expect to be heard. The marketers who are willing to listen to them will establish a significant competitive edge. Consumer empowerment and the Internet have profoundly changed consumer expectations, and another model must now be reflected in our channel mix.

That model is "customer engagement," which is based on the principle of *dialogue* rather than command. This marketing approach relies on a variety of nimble digital and offline media—such as Twitter, Facebook, customized Web pages, mobile, e-mail, blogs, forums, direct mail, and telemarketing driven by opt-in—to send the right message to the right individuals, at the right times, as determined by the *individual preferences of those consumers.*

> **WATCH OUT!**
>
> Focusing too closely on the specific technology necessary to establish customer engagement at any given moment is a mistake. These communication technologies are constantly in flux; a new one will doubtless have been born by the time this book is pub-

lished. What matters is not the name of the channel, or even its perceived newness or trendiness, but rather its capacity to facilitate a two-way dialogue. Even "old" technologies can be summoned to support this marketing model. The telephone, for instance, has provided the opportunity to engage in uniquely valuable person-to-person interactions for over a century, although (as the Do Not Call movement has demonstrated) it has not always been used in that way.

Figure 5.1 gives an example of a push marketing message sent to consumers by Ford Motor Company in 1914 via print advertising. It speaks simply and compellingly about the virtues of the Model T automobile: "Buy It Because It's a Better Car! Model T Touring Car: $650."

Of course, that's exactly the action the message wants us to take: to make our way to a car salesperson, lay our money down, and buy the Model T.

Figure 5.1: Ford Model T Touring Ad

A customer engagement marketing message sent by Ford Motor
Company in the year 2010, by contrast, might take one of the following forms:

- A YouTube video asking for viewer feedback.
- Twitter exchanges about experiences with Ford vehicles. Here's a
  sampling of recent (multiple) conversations:

  RT @tonyakeith: @Ford my daughter says her first car can't be a Ford
  because they're too nice to crash. (Priceless!)
  about 5 hours ago from OberTwitter

  @JackMad We've got lots of vehicles with 5-star crash ratings. Depends
  on what size you're looking for / what your needs are. ^SM
  about 2 hours ago from CoTweet in reply to JackiiMae

  @BarkBuckleUp awarded the 2010 Transit Connect the Top 10 Pet Safe
  Vehicle of Choice Award @ Chicago Auto Show! http://bit.ly/TransitFord
  about 2 hours ago from CoTweet

  Artist Scott Wade clearly favors the Ford Flex for his unique car art.
  Check out his stuff: http://cot.ag/aQBSs3
  about 2 hours ago from CoTweet

  We are honored that 2010 Flex has been selected as a @BarkBuckleUp
  Top 10 Pet Safe Vehicle of Choice! http://bit.ly/FlexFord
  about 2 hours ago from CoTweet

  Check out @BarkBuckleUp on 2010 Edge, which won the Top 10 Pet
  Safe Vehicle of @xxiinophobia What do you think about that inverted
  hood scoop? I just _ that! ^GP
  about 6 hours ago from CoTweet in reply to leynophobia

- A newsfeed updating subscribers about—and asking for feedback
  on—the latest chapter of "The Ford Story." Here's a snapshot of
  the (perpetually updated) story, available via www.at.ford.com:

FCN News: The Americas

Global | The Americas | Europe | Asia Pacific and Africa

MyFord Touch Defines Intuitive Driver Experience: Advanced Capabilities Voice-Controlled Now

Updated: Feb-10-2010 12:05 AM ET

CHICAGO—MyFord Touch driver connect technology, launching on the 2011 Ford Edge, is designed to be powerful yet intuitive for drivers, blending strengths of the most proven . . .

Feedback

We really value your feedback! Our goal is to continually improve this site, so please e-mail us your feedback.

- A message on Ford's Facebook page, which now boasts over 75,000 fans. Here's a recent example:

Ford Motor Company (Almost) final warning: Only 1 day left to apply to be a Ford Fiesta agent. Get those apps in! http://fiestamovement.com

16 minutes ago

Brent Tarlton Ford—send me a Fiesta to offset the carbon footprint of my 2010 GT500! In all seriousness though it would make for some good PR to have a GT500 owner drive one as his daily driver. I'd be more than happy to do that and share my experiences!

9 minutes ago · Report

In the example shown in Figure 5.1, the 1914 magazine advertisement, the information is simply "pushed" at the prospective consumer. In the 2010 examples, the consumer has the opportunity to engage with and communicate directly with the marketer via multiple channels—and to make preferences and requests (or demands!) known.

We believe that a successful multichannel marketing strategy now *must* include *customer engagement elements*. Failing to give customers an opportunity for direct and meaningful engagement with your company means yielding that immense strategic advantage to the competition!

In years past, we may have believed that we could simply *command* consumers into making *single* purchase decisions. Our channel mix today must accept the responsibility of *dialoguing* our way into a relationship that supports a *series* of purchase decisions.

Is push marketing dead? No. It is still a piece of the puzzle. It still has a role to play. If we expect push marketing alone to initiate conversations for us and win us long-term loyalty from consumers, however, we will be disappointed.

Action and reaction, ebb and flow, trial and error, change—this is the rhythm of living. Out of our overconfidence, fear; out of our fear, clearer vision, and fresh hope. And out of hope, progress.

—Bruce Barton

THE VOC CHANNEL MIX

Let's say that Melanie goes online during her lunch hour at work, and in a banner ad, she sees a Victoria's Secret promotion for a garment. She comes home and notices that she's received a mail order catalog; she reviews it with interest. That evening, a friend sends her a Facebook message about the Victoria's Secret sale. The next day, on her way to work, she passes a Victoria's Secret store, goes in and sees a sale *for a different item*—and buys it. What medium should get the credit for the purchase Melanie makes?

In this age of increasingly integrated media, does it really matter?

As we become better at multichannel marketing, measurement of the contribution of each individual medium will inevitably become harder. However, the overall results from these efforts have become increasingly easy to test and quantify. For example, the amount of increased spending and repeat spending by the population of customers who have received integrated, preference-driven multimedia communications can be measured against control groups that have not received these targeted communications. This is no longer a simplistic test of A versus B because of overarching factors such as retail presence and peer-to-peer communications, but it is still possible, and necessary, for us to identify, test, and measure the effect of different media combinations. That is the essence of our direct-marketing heritage.

To achieve this kind of synergy, and significant increases in response and revenue from our integrated multichannel deployment, we must rethink every element of the media mix. This applies to the new channels cited above and the traditional channels as well. Consider the following examples.

Multichannel action item: We must reconceive the role of inbound customer service call centers.

We must now deploy these customer service professionals as a *high-value customer interface*—and train and support them accordingly (see Figure 5.2).

By definition, inbound callers (even those calling in to complain) are more qualified and more likely to spend than others. However, what these inbound callers frequently encounter are human robots! Too many customers have become conditioned to poor service. This profoundly hurts their loyalty to the offending company. (We will cover this essential topic in much more depth in the later chapters on customer service.)

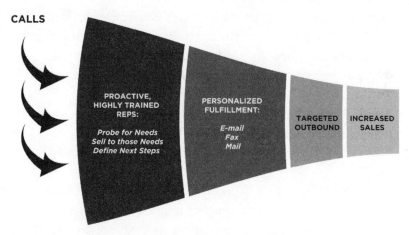

Figure 5.2: Inbound as a High-Value Experience

Multichannel action item: We must synchronize our outbound telemarketing and field sales reps with the rest of our channel deployment.

We must use VOC-driven preferences, as well as past interactions with individual customers or prospects, as the driving forces for our outbound and field sales initiatives. Otherwise, these proactive touches will become very annoying intrusions.

Outbound telemarketing salespeople must be trained in proactive, *service-oriented calls* to in-house telephone opt-in lists. Our experience is that these kinds of calls increase response by 500 to 700 percent when compared with direct-mail-only or e-mail-only efforts.

Similarly, field salespeople must be trained in disciplined *precall planning* and *relationship selling*. The days of "sell and disappear" are (thankfully) drawing to an end.

All of our field and phone sales efforts must be integrated with our other channel contact points for maximum responsiveness and cost-effectiveness. No, you don't have to accomplish this overnight. But yes, you must find a way to begin the process of changing your channel strategy, and upon doing that, you must broadcast the results to key stakeholders within your organization.

Multichannel action item: We must rethink direct mail as a high-value element of the channel mix.

In recent years, we have learned from VOC research, across many industries and company sizes, that direct mail is reemerging as a high-value medium. Here are the kinds of things we're hearing from both the business-to-business and business-to-consumer environments:

- "With the crushing amount of e-mail I get every day, not including the spam, I am in total e-mail 'overload.'"
- "Important information should be sent via direct mail, so it stands out."
- "It's about my time—I don't have the time to absorb or sort through all the junk. Mail implies importance."
- "At the end of the day I can't stand to look at my computer any longer. But I can take my stack of mail and peruse it at my leisure. It's actually kind of calming."
- "Mail is easier to share with other colleagues. It is also portable. I can bring it to meetings or someone's desk."

Based on these VOC findings, we feel that direct mail—a traditional push medium that has frequently operated in a world of its own—has a powerful role in today's multichannel media mix. However, there is a catch: direct mail should always be used as a highly personalized communication, driven (ideally) by the opt-in exchanges we've had with the customer. There is another catch, as well: it must deliver undeniably relevant communication. Most direct-mail offerings today do not meet these standards.

We believe that, in the twenty-first century, the direct-mail format should reflect clear, impossible-to-ignore value for the recipient and should include the following:

- A personalized letter, with targeted and relevant content
- Impact-addressed envelope, versus a label
- A live stamp

Postcard mailings are the antithesis of this and (not surprisingly) generate low return on investment (ROI).

Direct mail is effective at meaningful penetration of targeted markets and lists—ideally, opt-in lists. Some marketers seem to oppose direct mail on principle these days, but in a world increasingly dominated by multichannel purchase decisions, we believe that each channel's strengths—including direct mail—must be leveraged to increase results.

Direct Mail versus E-mail: The Winner Is Not Always a Given

One of the truly unfortunate trends in our industry is the tendency to dismiss direct mail altogether, on the grounds that it is, when compared to e-mail, too expensive, too slow, too outdated, or too "all of the above." Actually, though, like every other channel in today's ever-growing mix, direct mail has its role to play—assuming that it is used intelligently.

A client conducted a series of VOC-driven tests to measure the ROI of e-mail versus direct mail—given the prevailing view that e-mail drives the best ROI (see Figure 5.3).

In one version of the test, the client sent his message via e-mail. This was indeed cheap—it cost only 5 cents per solicitation (a figure that included all overhead, creative, and administrative costs). The e-mail

Finite Universe of Prospects: 50,000
Profit per unit sold: $200

	Direct Mail v2	Direct Mail v1	E-mail
Cost per solicitation	$5.00	$1.50	$0.05
Response rate (sales %)	10%	2%	0.13%
Cost per sale	$50.00	$75.00	$38.46
Total number of sales	5000	1000	65
Profit	$1,000,000	$200,000	$13,000

Can you run a business with 65 sales?

Figure 5.3: Direct Mail versus E-mail

pulled a 0.13 percent response. The cost per sale was $38. That would have been more than satisfactory if there had been a very large audience. But this was not the case. As it happened, there were only 50,000 prospects for this product at any one point in time. Therefore, total yield based on 0.13 percent response was 65 total sales and $13,000 profit. Notwithstanding a $38 cost per sale, the total yield of 65 purchasers would have meant disaster for my client who needed hundreds of buyers to achieve his goals.

That led us to option 2: a classic direct-mail piece. This ended up being significantly more expensive per piece than e-mail—30 times more expensive, or $1.50 per package, in the mail. As a result, the cost per sale doubled. Is that a bad thing? Not when response rate increased by almost 20 times, to 2 percent, and generated 1,000 customers from that finite universe of 50,000 potential buyers. It also drove a $200,000 profit.

Based on this success, a third approach was tested. This one was based on VOC feedback regarding the content, design, and feel of the package. It was elegant, elaborate, and expensive: $5 per package in the mail.

Thus, this package was roughly 100 times more expensive per piece than the e-mail. But, as it turned out, the cost per unit was not the only relevant metric!

The piece generated a fivefold increase in response over the prior direct-mail piece and almost a 100-fold increase over the response rate of the e-mail. This piece generated a 10 percent *response rate,* a rate most marketers only dream of. The cost per sale was actually lower than the prior mail package, and the piece generated 5,000 sales and $1,000,000 profit.

Note: Respondents in all three tests received personalized service calls after receipt of the e-mail or direct mail, and they were provided with links to a Web site for additional information, thus making this a multichannel, rather than exclusively a direct-mail-driven, campaign.

One moral of this story is that we can't just look at the expense of any given medium. We have to consider revenue based on yield and response rate. This client would have gone out of business using the e-mail-only model!

It's important to note that e-mail was an important part of follow-up to customers who bought, as were the Web site and customer service center. These provided important postsale information and customer support.

Another lesson is that high-value, VOC-driven direct mail, when used as part of a carefully crafted multichannel strategy, has a far higher impact than spray-and-pray direct mail. Most predictions about the demise of direct mail have failed to take into account just how powerful a truly targeted mail piece can be. The fact is, we notice when we receive a piece of mail that is clearly relevant to our own world. We get so much junk mail, and so many bills, that we can't help noticing when something is actually targeted to us as individuals. Far from being dead, *intelligent, multichannel-driven direct mail is today experiencing a heightened level of relevance and response.*

> Direct mail is not dead. It just needs to be driven by the Voice of the Customer and integrated as part of a multichannel strategy!

Multichannel action item: We must let the customer determine the frequency of communications received from us.

The channel mix must operate in accordance with timing and frequency that is determined by that individual's opt-in preferences. This is an ongoing engagement issue, and one whose metrics are likely to change over time. Regardless, we have an obligation to match up the timing of our messages with the ideal frequency for any given customer or prospect.

Multichannel action item: We must *integrate* the power of social media.

As you will see in the detailed Ford case study that appears in Chapter 7, social media can generate powerful results and deepen engagement via real-time conversations with customers and prospects. To integrate the power of social media, you must have at least one online spokesperson whose message matches up with the messages you send to customers and prospects. In the box "Scott Monty's Top 12 Tips for Becoming an Effective Online Spokesperson for Your Company," Ford's Scott Monty, from whom you'll hear much more in Chapter 7, offers some advice on this score.

SCOTT MONTY'S TOP 12 TIPS FOR BECOMING AN EFFECTIVE ONLINE SPOKESPERSON FOR YOUR COMPANY

Scott heads up the social media division for Ford Motor Company, which was cited in a recent national poll (conducted by Vitrue.com) as one of the 10 best in America. Scott's advice on establishing an effective online communication program appears below:

1. *Have the support of senior leadership.* If the senior-most people in your enterprise don't support the effort to engage with consumers one-on-one, that effort will not succeed. Show senior decision makers the latest evidence that social media is in fact an important marketing channel [this book is a good place to start] and get their blessing before you begin.

2. *Bring Legal in early and often.* Some attorneys will flinch at the very idea of company-sanctioned blog postings, Facebook accounts, and Twitter feeds; others will be intrigued and will want to take part, both as observers of what you are doing

and as participants in the discussion. Keep searching until you find someone in the second category and then build that person into your program from the very beginning. Talk regularly with Legal about what's safe to post and what's likely to lead to problems for your organization. Nothing should go out that surprises Legal.

3. *Establish your approach: branded, personal, or blended.* Your online "voice" can represent a nonpersonal "corporate" personality that reflects the branding message and reputation your company has established over the years; your online voice can represent a specific person (you) who speaks for the company, and has a unique personal history; or your online voice can be some combination of the two.

4. *Remind people that results are not instantaneous.* The program will take time to get off the ground and will be difficult to quantify. Even so, companies like Zappos, CNN, JetBlue, and (yes) Ford are making major investments in social media because it does have the potential to affect consumer perceptions in a profound way.

5. *Let people know that it's more than one person's job.* Engaging one-on-one with your organization's prospects and customers is a labor-intensive undertaking. You will need at least a small staff to get started.

6. *Listen first . . . and then listen some more.* Spend some time (virtual or face-to-face) with real, live customers and prospects. Hear them out, in depth, before you finalize your strategy or your message. These people will tell you what media you should be using to get involved, when to get involved, and with whom.

7. *Reply in context.* Complaints are going to come up; the question is how you will address them, and how rapidly. If you resolve to use social media to offer solutions and put a human face on the organization, you'll be able to translate the deeper issues the complaints are pointing you toward, and you'll be able to put even intense messages from your prospects and customers in the right perspective.

8. *Be respectful.* Always. No exceptions. No excuses. Your corner of cyberspace cannot become a shouting zone.
9. *Have resources at the ready.* This is one of the reasons it's so important to have buy-in from senior decision makers as you launch the program. If your online program gives consumers the opportunity to vent about a problem, but it is seen as offering no solutions, it will not make a positive impression. You must have the resources necessary to address the most common issues that arise, and authority to use those resources.
10. *Remember: You're always on the record.* The Internet is an unforgiving place. Anything you say can come back to haunt both your enterprise and you. If you have doubts about the wisdom of a certain course of action—check with Legal.
11. *Have a sense of humor.* This job can actually be fun—if you let it.
12. *Don't take things personally.* This is not about you. Once people are done blowing off steam, make it clear that your job is to stay connected to continue the discussion. Before long, that fact alone will be enough to get people to sit up and take notice of the good things your company is doing.

The very definition of a BtoB or BtoC "market leader" will soon include a robust, and constantly evolving, social media initiative. With greater and greater predictability, the Voice of the Customer is telling us that a good portion of the customer's conversation with us now needs to take place by means of interactive social media channels like forums, blogs, Facebook, and Twitter. We are missing huge opportunities for engagement if we ignore those trends. Many organizations, such as Ford, have capitalized on the trend, and they have achieved remarkable results by incorporating direct discussions with consumers into the marketing mix.

Ford is by no means alone in acknowledging the importance of using social media as a marketing, customer service, and public relations channel. (As we shall see, these three disciplines frequently overlap in the online world.) David Carr of the *New York Times* recently wrote of a cross-country plane trip he took on Virgin America, which offers in-flight Internet access. During the voyage, Carr made a casual remark, via Twitter, about his seatmate on the flight, whom he described as "the leader of a cult involving Axe body spray." Thirty minutes later, a Virgin America steward materialized and tactfully offered Carr the opportunity to switch seats! Clearly, someone at Virgin was closely monitoring, and responding to, consumer tweets that mentioned the company, a best practice that now seems essential. That best practice resulted, in this case, in the kind of free publicity whose value is hard to calculate! There are literally thousands of such stories. We can like Twitter or dislike it, but its impact as a channel for improving relationships with customers now seems indisputable.

> Mobile phones with text messaging capability now represent an essential communication channel with consumers. Consider the Red Cross campaign that used text messages from cellular phones to raise over $22 million in a matter of days to support relief efforts following the earthquake in Haiti, an appeal in partnership with the National Football League that raised over $500,000 an hour at its peak (Source: *New York Times*, January 18, 2010).
>
> A similarly intriguing result was posted by Chicago's Shedd Aquarium, which ran a test in its television ads to see which medium drew the most interactions with consumers: a Web site or an SMS code for text messaging. Although the text code appeared in only one quarter of the ads, it delivered over three times the total response of the Web address (Source: *1to1 Magazine*).

Multichannel action item: We must deploy all of our communications according to the customer's preferences.

The multichannel mix must be deployed at the appropriate points in our customer's life cycle and according to their preferences. That means our communications should be driven by the opt-in preferences we've determined by one of two methods: either in-depth Voice-of-the-Customer interviews or careful analysis of the actual behavioral trends of customers over time.

Acquisition of customers is important, of course, but the retention of customers is equally or more important, and it is a topic that is frequently overlooked by marketers. When we analyze the reasons behind high churn rates (or high inactivity rates), we tend to find that the reason is a problem in either channel strategy, or channel execution, that has taken us out of alignment with the Voice of the Customer.

Of course, this is a lot for anyone to take on, and a lot for any organization to process. No one is asking you to turn your company upside down, and no one is insisting that you use all of your existing marketing channels as platforms for hourlong conversations with all of your customers. What does have to change, though, is the way we *think about* multichannel strategy. That's the essential first step. We think the goal of that strategy should be to fulfill the requirements articulated by your customers in the course of interacting with built-in VOC "feedback loops."

Integrated multichannel marketing can achieve its potential to drive double-digit results only if the media mix is deployed according to the opt-in preferences of our customers and prospects. Otherwise, marketers are only achieving multichannel spray-and-pray irritation.

These feedback loops are essential. Think of the VOC Relationship Research as something we conduct *up front,* to reengineer our customer engagement strategies. Our work doesn't stop there, however. We must keep informing ourselves about the ever-changing needs of our customers. The vehicles for this ongoing feedback include our customer service reps, our blogs, our forums, Facebook pages, and so on. *This ongoing and ever-deepening understanding of our customers provides the qualitative and quantitative feedback we need to guide effective decisions regarding new channels, value propositions, offers, messages, and so on.*

Thus, synchronizing our marketing channels around the demands of the customer, as uncovered by an ongoing VOC feedback program, is a never-ending strategic imperative, not a one-time quick fix.

Isolated touch points will always lack the impact of an orchestrated multichannel deployment. A tightly synchronized, integrated marketing campaign, on the other hand, will enable all components of the multichannel mix to work together as a unified force—and deliver critical information from engaged consumers that is unavailable from any other source.

AN EXAMPLE OF HOW THREADLESS USED THE VOICE OF THEIR CUSTOMERS TO DRIVE STRATEGIC MULTICHANNEL DISTRIBUTION DECISIONS

Threadless is a leading community-centered online apparel seller that engages with artists, consumers, and others to create innovative T-shirt designs. You'll learn more about Threadless in Chapter 8.

> We listen to our community members and make decisions based on their opinions. Of course, there may be widely diverging opinions among community members, but in general, if the community at large feels strongly for or against something, we take that into consideration. An example is the distribution of our products through other retailers. We had been considering distributing our products more broadly through various third-party brick-and-mortar retailers. At the same time, we had also been approached by a massive retailer. We thought that this particular partner wouldn't be a good brand fit for us, and we expected to pass on the opportunity, but we also wanted to confirm the wishes of the community. We asked the community members what they felt, and in general, what we heard confirmed our belief that working with this large retailer just wouldn't be the right move for us. However, we also learned a lot about other places that members of our community felt distributing our products could make sense.
>
> —Thomas V. Ryan, CEO, Threadless

CASE STUDY:
DISNEY DESTINATIONS

C O M P A N Y B R I E F I N G
FROM CRM TO CMR
WALT DISNEY COMPANY
TOM C. BOYLES, Senior Vice President,
Global Customer Managed Relationships

Our goal at the Disney theme parks and resorts is pretty simple: We are trying to create the best guest experience in the world.

The focus, from senior management right down to the cast member who actually interacts with the guest, is on being what we call "guest-centric," which means that we put the guest at the center of our universe. Frankly, I don't know of another organization that's more focused on the guest than we are.

We're trying to synchronize a lot of channels together, including TV, print, direct mail, e-mail, Web sites, search engines, alliance partners, promotions, and even some new channels we haven't formalized our plans on yet. All of that synchronization is in support of one thing: a great guest experience. That experience could be an online game, an interaction with one of our agents over the phone, a direct-mail piece, or a visit to one of our parks. At the same time, we recognize that we live in a world where the guest has more say over what is going to be experienced, and when it is going to be experienced, than ever before. That's why we feel that the driving principle always has to be that the guest is in charge of what happens—in every channel.

Changing the Terminology

In keeping with that goal, we made an important change in our own internal terminology. We decided that, even though the common phrase "customer relationship management"—CRM—encompasses the idea that you can interact and function with the guest, it really didn't say that in a way that made us happy from a Disney perspective. Although CRM is certainly important, we replaced it with the phrase "customer managed relationship"—CMR. This term reinforces the notion of the guest being the one who is driving the experience. That's our ideal, across multiple channels. Our job is to share information internally and integrate those channels in a way that helps the guest make good decisions.

In support of CMR, the customer managed relationship, we revised a critical internal goal that we'd been pursuing for some time: "Know the guest and be relevant." While that's still an essential concept for us, one that we come back to every day, we've gotten much more specific with it in recent years. Now we see our job as follows: "Know the guest well enough, at any point in time or place, that we know what to do next." After all, for "Know me and be relevant" to work, the guest has to be willing to engage with us in a manner that actually allows us to help him or her!

The Three-Part Standard

Look closely at how each part of that updated standard works, on both the practical and emotional level.

Know the guest well enough . . .

Do We Know . . .

the preferred channels for communication with this person?

the nature of the last direct contact?

the number of past stays at a Disney property?

the date of the last visit?

the demographics? (Parents with young children? Grandparents with young children? Visitors with no children?)

the resort last visited?

the preferred travel dates?

this person's favorite Disney character?

what the prior dining choices were?

the reason for the last visit?

the reason for this visit?

And so on.

. . . at any point in time or place . . .

Is This Person . . .

online researching the details about one of our resorts?

checking pricing?

talking with one of our agents on the phone?

at the front gate?

interacting with a cast member right now?

checking into a resort?

looking for his or her favorite character?

And so on.

. . . that we know what to do next.

Is the Right Thing to Do Next to . . .

do *Nothing*? (For instance: Do we really want to send a text message to this person's cell phone when we know he or she is at Epcot Center, enjoying a show?)

provide the guest's information to the cast members who will be interacting with him or her?

recommend a resort, ticket, or package?

offer an alternative week?

direct the guest to a specific attraction?

suggest open table seating?

offer an update on wait times?

As an internal decision-making tool, this three-part standard is indispensable. If an initiative doesn't allow us to improve in one or more of these three areas, we don't invest in it unless we absolutely have no other choice. A lot of those investments have involved finding better ways to share information internally at Disney about the guest.

Sharing Internal Information

A decade ago, we had all of our data systems structured in such a way that they rolled up in a silo fashion; there was no really good distribution of information about the guests. The information we had in a booking system was not connected to the dining system, or the ticket system, or any of the other component pieces. As a result, we were often working in an information vacuum when we interacted with a guest.

Today, thanks to some exponential advances in information technology, we are in a position to share much more information with our own people across functional areas. We've tried to do this in a way that supports engagement with the guest, allows us to do the "next right thing," and leaves the guest in charge of the overall experience. We have a saying: "No one owns the guest, but someone always owns the moment." In other words, no one person or department is responsible for the entirety of the guest experience, but someone on the Disney side is always responsible for any given moment the guest encounters.

The real beauty of today's technology is that it allows you to share emotionally powerful information gathered from an individual—information someone gives you about, say, a favorite Disney character—and then appeal to that information at various points throughout the relationship, whenever and wherever you engage with that person.

For instance: *The Little Mermaid* is a pivotal point in my life with my daughter. It was the first film she and I went to see together. So whenever I see that film today, or hear the music from the film, or see still images from the film, what do you think happens to me? I go into a positive emotional state! Well, if I mention that Ariel is one of my favorite characters to you during an online exchange, you can leverage that information. You can appeal to the character Ariel during my voice-to-voice contact with you. If you do that, the odds are very good that I'm going to have a powerful positive emotional response to you, and to our entire exchange. What's more, if the next person I talk to, a week later, can help me build Ariel into the discussion, my engagement is going to get even stronger. And if my daughter and I interact with Ariel in real time as the day moves along, then very likely, I'm going to have a positive response to the whole day. All because you chose to engage with me about something that matters to me, and each touch point supports me as I make choices that deepen the emotional experience.

That's the kind of thing today's information technology allows us to do: leverage information from multiple channels, so that we can connect with guests on an emotionally compelling level. Of course, we can connect not just about character preferences but also about other emotionally powerful issues within a household, such as anniversaries and birthdays and children.

Interestingly, a great deal of emotion connects to the issue of when not to communicate with a guest: learning when not to reach out, based on the individual preferences of the guest, actually has significant economic value. In today's brave new world, where the guests really are in charge, you don't want to be perceived as using any channel for spamming the household or sending irrelevant messaging. Ignoring a consumer's preferences carries a very high cost. It may mean that the consumer chooses to reject you and turn you off—while they'll let others in.

Consumers Must Choose to Let You In

The kind of engagement that gets individuals to choose to let you in, that gets them to look forward to hearing from you, has become more and more possible for us to support in recent years. In large measure, that's because of the merging of the digital, physical, and virtual worlds that has taken place. In my view, this change is unlike anything that's ever happened in the past, and it's certainly had a huge impact on the way we operate.

A decade ago, it was almost like the guest was three or four different people to us. There was one database for you when you were on the property, and another for when you responded to an e-mail message, and another that connected to you when you responded to direct mail, and so forth. Those worlds didn't really connect. Now it's a very different situation. We can use the digital space to communicate with you, and when you come on to a property, the agents will know about what you've already chosen to share with us online. Often, that's quite a lot of information because of the explosion of interest in the virtual world that has taken place. We now have information that's been shared by millions of people from immersive experiences on the Internet, from social media, and from countless online communities. It's important to understand that our use of this information isn't something we're pushing on people; it's part of the customer's expectation of us in the twenty-first century.

Basically, people are now saying to us, "Okay, I want to be known in your digital world, and then I also want you to know me when I come into your physical world, and then I want to be able to leverage the information that I've given you in the virtual world, in whatever way, manner, and shape I choose to do that." That's the expectation of the customer managed relationship. Meeting that expectation, and using it to deliver the world's best guest experience through multiple channels, is what we're working on here.

An engagement model, like the customer managed relationship model we use, carries a huge advantage over other models because it allows you to start with the consumer. That's important for us because the Disney offerings are so vast that it actually makes much more sense to start with the individual if you can do that. There's such a rich variety of offerings here that you could, if you wanted to, come here and play golf, take a spa, visit some of the best restaurants on the Eastern seaboard, and never set foot in the park. By the same token, you can spend time in the park from nine o'clock in the morning until midnight, and you can fill the whole day with attractions and everything else that you'll find in that environment. Our job is to figure out how to be relevant to the guest's choices in any permutation of those spaces, whether the guest is planning the visit, actually coming on to the property, or engaging with us online after the visit.

From the Guest's Perspective

So what does all this look like to the guest? Well, let's say you're in a family that's been thinking of a visit to one of our theme parks. You respond to a TV ad, and you call us, and you book the visit. A customized welcome mailer will go out no later than 24 hours after your contact with our call center. This truly is "direct mail," as in customer-specific mail: every paragraph of copy, every headline, every photo is relevant to your household and derived from our conversation with you, and it is based on a database that is updated continuously based on every new contact we've had with you.

Now let's suppose that you connected with us last night about a vacation, but you didn't book your trip. You will get a customized DVD that connects to the content that your household—not any other household, but yours—shared with us about the Disney vacation you're contemplating. This DVD also incorporates what you told us last night about the period when you wanted to make the trip, and the resort where you were considering staying. Not only that, it highlights a customized Target Week that can help you take advantage of a discount that matches up with your schedule.

Eventually, if you book a stay at one of our resorts, you'll also get a mailing that's specific to that location and highlights photos and text that are specific to the resort you're staying in. The mailing will integrate all the information you've shared with us so far, no matter where you were when you shared it with us.

In fact, the whole sequence of contacts is unique to the individual user. It is tailored to what you've told us about your family through all the channels where we've been interacting with you. And all of these "touches" through the various channels perform three jobs: they elicit new information from a brand-new channel experience; they help us to reinforce the initial preferences you've already shared with us; and they also move the discussion to the next level, allowing us to make new recommendations about experiences and venues based on what you've already shared. We are integrating the various channels to feed relevant information and options back to you continuously—as you make the decisions.

Disney: The Takeaways

Ideally, every channel interaction is harmonized with every other channel interaction. Ideally, every call-center exchange, every piece of mail you receive from us, every e-mail that shows up from us in your inbox, every game you play with us online, is built around this idea of our knowing you well enough to be relevant to a specific time and place, and thus knowing what to do next. If we are relevant, if we're doing the right things for you, if we're listening to what you've said and working that into what we're doing, then we believe that you will not only visit but that you will come back and visit us again.

The Results

Since 2000, we have increased our contribution from channel marketing initiatives by 3.5 times. This was accomplished by the following:

- Growing the database by over 100 percent
- Increasing our number of targeted interactions by over 10 times
- Expanding our e-mail coverage by over 10 times
- Creating and/or enabling relevant and timely guest communications, offers, and services through multiple channels

---

NOW WHAT?

Do a company self-check. How many of these six multichannel requirements for the new millennium have you implemented?

1. The optimal deployment of media should be driven by VOC learnings to ensure both relevance and effectiveness.
2. Key elements of the multichannel mix must be deployed according to the individual opt-in preferences of customers and prospects.
3. The multichannel mix must provide customers and/or prospects with choices so they can communicate with the marketer via the media mix of their choice.
4. The channel mix must meet requirements 1 through 3 above in accordance with the timing and frequency determined by that individual's opt-in preferences.
5. The channel mix must offer a completely integrated experience. All the elements must complement each other, support each other, and send coordinated messages to customers and prospects.
6. The channel mix must be responsive. If the organization alienates or abuses a consumer, we can expect to hear about it in a public forum if we do not resolve it privately.

Don't stop here! In the next chapter, you'll learn how to develop creative multichannel initiatives that truly engage the customer.

CHAPTER 6

ADDITIONAL BEST-IN-CLASS MULTICHANNEL LEADERS YOU CAN LEARN FROM

EXECUTIVE SUMMARY

The case studies in this chapter illustrate how VOC-driven multichannel strategies can help organizations achieve the following:
- Turn customers into evangelists, as Nike has proven.
- Deliver 60 percent market share while competing with a global powerhouse, as SCA has achieved.
- Improve renewal rates by nearly 20 percent, as HMS has proven.

In this chapter, you'll see additional real-world examples of how companies have listened closely to their customers and then used what they've learned to implement powerful multichannel programs.

CASE STUDY:
NIKE TAKES MULTICHANNEL TO ANOTHER LEVEL

CLOSE-UP ON NIKE
- Headquarters: Beaverton, Oregon
- Major U.S. manufacturer of athletic shoes, apparel, and sports equipment
- Approximately 30,000 employees
- www.nike.com

When it comes to innovative business-to-consumer multichannel campaigns, footwear manufacturer Nike is in a league of its own.

The Nike+iPod Sport Kit

Consider its groundbreaking 2006 partnership with Apple to launch the Nike+iPod Sport Kit—a wireless system that actually allows a runner's Nike footwear to communicate with his or her iPod, thus delivering an enhanced running and workout experience. "We're working with Nike to take music and sport to a new level," said Steve Jobs, Apple's CEO at the time of the product launch. "The result is like having a personal coach or training partner motivating you every step of your workout."

And, he might have added, a couple of million running buddies. On August 31, 2008, over 700,000 Nike+ users worldwide took part in a 10-kilometer run that Nike called the Human Race. Runners logged over 4 million miles—and uploaded the data to prove it.

According to Nike, "Information on time, distance, calories burned, and pace is stored on iPod and displayed on the screen; real-time audible feedback also is provided through headphones. The kit includes an in-shoe sensor and a receiver that attaches to iPod." Direct engagement with the consumer has rarely been so direct.

Not surprisingly, the Nike-Apple alliance has also been the subject of an intense social media campaign. Exhibit 1 in Nike's multichannel suite is the system's official Facebook page, and it boasts over 3,000 fans; a Twitter feed, @nikeplus, is similarly active. The Nike+ community is an essential part of both brand experiences (Apple's and Nike's).

A campaign to help victims of the 2010 Haiti earthquake, for instance, elicited the support of thousands of Nike+ users. Take a look at what one of them wrote in a blog, and notice how quickly she fast-forwards over her (minor) technical complaints with the device to spread the word about the company's high-profile charity initiative:

WHEN THE VOICE OF THE CUSTOMER IS THE VOICE OF THE EVANGELIST

Help for Haiti: Join the @nikeplus Challenge—
Nike Donating $1 for Every Mile/Kilometer Run
Join Nike in helping rebuild Haiti after the earthquake by committing your Nike+ runs to the effort. By doing so, you will be helping Nike raise up to $100,000 as part of their overall commitment to donate $500,000 to the efforts in Haiti. $1 will be donated for every mile/kilometer run with a goal of reaching 100,000 miles or 160,000 kilometers. For more info visit www.nike.com/haiti.

I'm a member of Nike+, and while I had occasional struggles with the device, the Web site and social aspects of the site have never let me down. . . . Users can create their own groups and challenges to spur on more running (and more purchases of the Nike+ device and membership in the site), individual members can establish goals for themselves (resulting in recurrent visits and stickiness), and there's even integrated chat called "Trash Talk," which allows members to broadcast their thoughts and opinions to the group.

This latest endeavor—Help for Haiti—is another brilliant execution by Nike. It's a call to action to run more with the Nike+ device because not only will it benefit yourself, but it will benefit those in need in Haiti. I've been feeling especially lazy after returning from Hawaii (plus, I'm still nursing my pulled muscle), but this encourages me to get out there as soon as possible. Every mile counts. For me. And for them.
—Kathy Johnson, Kathy Johnson's Personal Blog,
posted February 2, 2010, katson.blogspot.com/
2010/02/help-for-haiti-join-nikeplus-challenge.html

What you just read may well be a glimpse of the future of multi-channel marketing: empowered, engaged consumers advocating on behalf of a marketer whose products, services, and values align with their own. The lesson: *Use your channel mix to enlist customers and prospects in a cause that matches both your values, and theirs.*

Exhibit 2 in the innovative Nike multichannel suite would be NIKEiD, a breathtaking (and surprisingly affordable) online application enabling Nike customers to design their own footwear and to view it in three stunning dimensions before placing an order. The technology effectively fuses brand and channel: once you're done designing the perfect pair of running shoes, you can post your design work on (you guessed it) a Facebook page, where other do-it-yourself designers are waiting to critique your work (Figure 6.1).

One user chose a pink motif, and then shared the resulting footwear with all her family and friends via e-mail. Talk about consumer engagement!

Nike also built a fashionable London boutique around the NIKEiD design-it-yourself process—which is, I warn you ahead of time, addictive.

Figure 6.1: A Nike Customer Posts His Footwear Design on Facebook

The Results

> The bottom line on Nike's innovative multichannel initiative: 61 percent market share

Not long ago, Adweek Media announced the winners of its Best of the 2000s advertising awards, and the Nike-Apple collaboration showed up as one of the winners. The Nike+ project was chosen as the Digital Campaign of the Decade. According to Adweek Media, the program was cited as the kind of initiative that "defined how a brand can build a self-sustaining platform" via the Nike+iPod receiver. Given its sustained emphasis on a unique, highly engaging "product experience," it's no surprise that Nike has increased its share of the running shoes market from 48 percent (2006) to 61 percent (2008). So far, Nike+ users have put in a staggering 100 million miles using Nike+iPod.

CASE STUDY:
SCA GOES LOCAL, CHALLENGES GOLIATH

CLOSE-UP ON SCA
- Headquarters: Stockholm, Sweden
- Located in 60 countries
- Annual sales in 2009 amounted to 11.3 billion euros
- Products include personal-care products, tissue, packaging, publication papers, and solid-wood products in more than 90 countries
- www.sca.com

Libero's Multichannel Marketing Strategies

Perhaps you're wondering if you need a "hot" product—like smart sneakers—to put an integrated multichannel strategy to work? The following case study, which comes from the Swedish personal-care products manufacturer SCA, proves otherwise. The product in question? Diapers. The market? Denmark. The competition? Goliath—in the form of Procter & Gamble.

In the Nordic region of Europe, the children's diaper market is mature. The growth of the customer base is severely limited due to low birth rates. That means all growth in market share must come from a comparatively small group of users—a group that is constantly changing.

"Our target group is the total market of diaper users in the region," explained Pernille Thorslund Kyhl, Nordic direct marketing manager for Libero, the diaper division. "One-third of the target group changes each year, as the children outgrow the need for diapers at the age of three. The consumers are only in the target group for a limited time. We need to win them early and keep them loyal to get the full potential from each consumer. We believe the best way to do that is share our own status as parents and offer advice, insights, and ideas as one parent to another—and let the best solution be chosen by the parent because he or she is closest to the child and knows what is best."

Libero uses a wide range of channels to communicate and influence the target group—channels so creatively selected and deployed that it has actually outmaneuvered the global personal-care giant Procter & Gamble, whose Pampers brand ranks second in the region.

The innovative Libero channel mix—the direct result of the marketers' own direct experience as parents and their interactions with other parents—breaks down as follows:

Libero is the publisher of a hugely popular—and free—pregnancy book entitled *Pregnancy, Delivery, and the New Family* that equates roughly, in terms of authoritativeness and influence, to the American classic *What to Expect When You're Expecting*. Libero's volume is distributed gratis to the majority of pregnant women in the region by a trusted source: the woman's own personal doctor. Obviously, this branded gift takes place at a critical moment in the woman's life. The combination of great advice, perfect timing, and impeccable personal endorsement gives Libero impossible-to-beat positioning as a trustworthy brand.

Libero works with a huge network of midwives to get the best possible distribution of Libero diapers within hospitals.

Libero has a major presence in professional fairs that serve midwives and nurses and is active in supporting the educational needs of these critical-care providers to pregnant women and new mothers.

Libero also runs the popular Libero Club, whose purpose is to increase loyalty among members. The club uses e-mail and Internet communication to deliver rewards to loyal users—and keep in touch with parents who move to new locations. The Libero Club is a classic example of opt-in self-profiling: parents share family details with the company in exchange for a clearly defined set of benefits, which include not only coupons for additional products but also authoritative information on subjects of interest to the family, such as the skin-care needs of infants or the best ways to reduce the environmental impact of disposable diapers.

Libero also uses print, Internet, outdoor advertising, and television commercials to build the brand, reinforce existing purchasing patterns, keep brand awareness high, and recruit to the Libero Club.

Notice that this channel mix uses conventional push marketing channels to support an array of high-engagement channels. The Libero mix is not only extremely creative; it's also virtually impossible to duplicate within the target market. The key constituencies—including the critical channels of doctors and midwives—are interconnected in such a way as to prevent any competitor attempting to displace SCA. Midwives in the region have an extremely strong relationship with the company and its brand; so do doctors; and so, of course, do parents.

Kyhl told us: "All of our communications with the target groups are designed not simply to sell product but also to help parents and caregivers. It is part of our mission to give them support and useful information on an individual basis. We care for, and are genuinely interested in, our consumers. I think this is what makes a huge difference in the quality of our relationships with them."

All of our communications with the target groups are designed not simply to sell product but also to help parents and caregivers. It is part of our mission to give them support and useful information on an individual basis. We care for, and are genuinely interested in, our consumers. I think this is what makes a huge difference in the quality of our relationships with them.

—PERNILLE THORSLUND KYHL,
NORDIC DIRECT MARKETING MANAGER, LIBERO

The high quality of those relationships is reflected in the company's strong competitive position. SCA's Libero brand, which started with a 6 percent share in Denmark, is today the market leader in an intensely competitive market. The company's staggering 60 percent market share, posted in direct competition with globally dominant Procter & Gamble, is the direct result of a world-class channel mix that engages, creates unique relationships with, and serves the parents and caregivers in the region.

The Takeaways

- Place more importance on being interested than on being interesting.
- Engage locally. This is the only reliable way to beat worldwide brands; their systems simply can't compete with strong local relationships.
- Individualize communication with consumers and key allies.

CASE STUDY:
HMS NATIONAL UPS THE ANTE

CLOSE-UP ON HMS NATIONAL
- Founded in 1983
- *Mission statement:* "We stand for peace of mind . . . for real estate professionals who appreciate our reputation for service and reliability . . . for home buyers who want protection against unexpected repair costs on home appliances and systems . . . and for home sellers who leverage the HMS Home Warranty to help sell their homes."
- www.hmsnational.com

HMS National Extends Its Lead

HMS National, Inc., is a 30-year-old company that markets and sells home warranties through real estate agents. HMS's home warranties help homeowners avoid unexpected bills for repair and replacements that can often be quite expensive. These warranties provide coverage for mechanical failures of many major systems and appliances, including air-conditioning and heating systems, refrigerators, washers, dryers, ovens, electrical systems, and more. Thus, HMS offers coverage that is normally not provided by most homeowners' insurance policies.

These warranties are frequently initiated either when a home is listed for sale or at the time of a home's purchase. The warranty contract is typically annual, and at the end of the year, the consumer faces a key decision: to renew or not to renew?

Douglas Stein, president of HMS, wanted to increase renewal rates. But before developing an action plan, he wanted insights regarding customers' needs and expectations so he could develop the most effective strategies. According to Doug: "At HMS, our culture is one of continual improvement. Although our renewal marketing program was successful, we wanted to take our results to the next level. I felt it was essential to build our effort around further understanding our customers' needs and expectations. We could then use that detail to refine our end-to-end customer experience. To meet the goals I had set for the company, it was important to be comprehensive in our approach, but also to achieve results quickly—ideally within six months."

As a result, the goals of the VOC Relationship Research Process were twofold:

- Significantly increase renewal rates.
- Refine the customer experience across multiple channels.

As Doug Stein put it: "The guiding principle for the VOC objectives was to learn as much as we could about HMS customers' needs . . . and then use that knowledge to drive all of our new marketing and renewal initiatives."

These were the objectives for the VOC research:

- Identify what a home warranty actually meant to customers.
- Determine how customers defined the value of HMS.
- Evaluate the experiences customers were having in the claims process, and spotlight specific strengths and identify if any weaknesses existed.
- Measure the customers' overall level of satisfaction with HMS.
- Analyze perceptions of HMS's marketing communications.
- Gain insights into possible product enhancements.

- Determine customers' willingness to opt-in and self-profile preferences to drive targeted communications.

The VOC research sample was structured around two major groups: customers who renewed and customers who didn't. Within each of these groups, we identified four important subgroups for in-depth research interviews: home buyers who had purchased a home warranty from HMS; home sellers who had purchased a home warranty from HMS; homeowners who had filed a claim; and homeowners who had not filed a claim.

The following were some of the learnings that emerged from the research.

- Regardless of who actually purchased the warranty—the home seller or the home buyer—overall customer engagement was an area for improvement. Prior to this point, HMS's initial touch point with customers—a fulfillment package—was informational and factual without being particularly engaging (Figure 6.2). The VOC research

HOME WARRANTY AGREEMENT

This Home Warranty Agreement, hereinafter referred to as the "Agreement", is marketed through HMS National, Inc. The Agreement is issued by the entity listed for your state in Section VII. 11. of this Agreement. Such entity is hereinafter referred to as the "Issuing Company", or "we", "us", and/or our". The owner of the home covered by this Agreement is hereinafter referred to as "you" and/or "your". This is a Home Warranty Agreement, not an insurance policy.

This Agreement is intended to provide protection against the cost of repairing certain types of mechanical failures of specific items in your home. **Please read the Agreement carefully. Coverage includes only certain mechanical failures of the specific items listed as covered on your Agreement Coverage Summary and excludes all other failures and/or items. The Agreement Coverage Summary is attached to and made a part of this Agreement.** Coverage is subject to the limitations and conditions specified in this Agreement.

I. TYPES OF WARRANTIES/EFFECTIVE DATES

Your Agreement type, effective date and expiration date are listed on your Agreement Coverage Summary. Types of warranties are as follows:
1. **A Seller Home Warranty**, which is placed on the home by a prospective home seller at or near the time of listing, is effective immediately upon receipt and processing of the Seller Home Warranty application by us and continues for the remaining term of the listing agreement, not to exceed one hundred and eighty (180) days from the date of listing, unless sooner terminated by the sale of the dwelling (see Buyer Conversion Warranty below) or cancellation of the listing agreement. The Seller Home Warranty may be extended by us at our sole discretion. The Seller Home Warranty converts to a Buyer Conversion Warranty (see below) on the date of closing (title transfer), provided required payment has been received by us within seven (7) business days of closing.
2. **A Buyer Conversion Warranty**, which is a Seller Home Warranty that has converted to benefit a home buyer after closing, is effective on the date of closing, provided required payment has been received by us within seven (7) business days of closing.
3. **A Buyer Direct Warranty**, which is purchased by or on behalf of a home buyer at the time of closing, is effective on the date of closing, provided required payment has been received by us within seven (7) business days of closing, unless otherwise agreed to by us in writing.
4. **A New Home Warranty**, which is purchased by or on behalf of a home buyer at the time of closing of a newly constructed single family home. Coverage becomes effective on the 366th day from the date of closing, and continues for three years from that date, provided required payment has been received by us within seven (7) business days of closing, unless otherwise agreed to by us in writing.
5. **An Open Direct Warranty**, which is available to homeowners not immediately purchasing or selling their home (i.e., when the home is not listed for sale and/or it is more than seven (7) business days after closing), is effective thirty (30) days after required payment has been received by us, unless we otherwise agree in writing.

II. BASIS FOR COVERAGE

We agree to pay the covered costs to repair or replace the items listed as covered on your Agreement Coverage Summary if any such items become inoperable during the term of this Agreement due to mechanical failure caused by routine wear and tear, subject to the terms and conditions of this Agreement. Determination of coverage for any claim will be made solely by us, considering but not limited to, our independent contractor's diagnosis. We reserve the right, at our option, to replace items rather than repair them. The definitions of the specific items that may be listed on your Agreement Coverage Summary as covered, as well as other limitations on coverage and other terms and conditions, are listed below.

This Agreement covers only mechanical failures relating to the mechanical parts and components of those domestic-grade items that were in the home and in proper operating condition on the Agreement effective date. "Mechanical failure" occurs when a covered item becomes inoperable and unable to perform its designed function, subject to the limitations and conditions set forth herein. HMS will cover a pre-existing mechanical failure provided the failure could not have been detected by visual inspection or simple mechanical test. A visual inspection of the covered item is considered to mean the viewing of an item to verify that it appears structurally intact and without damage or missing parts that would indicate inoperability. A simple mechanical test means the ability to turn the unit off and on verifying the item operates without irregular sounds or smoke that may indicate a problem. In certain instances, we may require documentation from you during a claim review.

Figure 6.2: HMS National's Fulfillment Package Prior to the VOC Research

Source: HMS National

revealed that this initial communication was a critical point in the relationship. The materials the company used to welcome its new customers (and, of course, lay the groundwork for the eventual renewal decision) could be better aligned to match customers' needs.

- The quality of the customers' claims experiences had a significant effect on renewal behavior. Interestingly, with HMS's solid, caring customer experience, satisfaction was typically quite high, even if the claim amounts paid to the consumers were not the exact amounts they had expected. By the same token, even when HMS paid out significantly more than expected on a claim, customer satisfaction about the claim experience remained an important factor regarding renewal.

- Real estate agents were major drivers of the customers' perceptions of the value of renewing their warranties. This finding was critical because it identified a previously unaddressed channel opportunity.

In addition, the VOC research identified other important opportunities that profoundly impacted HMS's marketing strategies. For instance, it was learned that there were opportunities for refining the HMS customer experience; that HMS could help customers more fully understand and calculate the value of a warranty (a critical concern for homeowners considering renewal); and that consumers were receptive to the prospect of self-profiling their interests and contact preferences, once they understood the value of doing so.

"Customers told us," Doug recalled, "that they would be willing to share information with HMS regarding their homes, interests, and preferences—if they were certain that this information would be used to create a customized experience and communications that would deliver meaningful value to them."

This finding emphasizes one of the central themes of this book: **Customers must understand the *value* they will receive from populating an opt-in database with their preference information. They expect that this information will be used to drive relevant and personally useful information and/or resources to them.**

In the VOC research, customers told HMS that sources of additional value would include important information such as maintenance tips, that is, simple steps they could take to reduce the frequency and cost of problems with boilers, HVAC systems, plumbing systems, and so on. However, these had to be personalized to their home and the equipment contained in their home. Otherwise, this information would be viewed as generic and of low value.

Deploying the Multichannel Mix

The insights from the VOC research helped lay the groundwork for HMS to develop more effective strategies in a number of areas. For instance:

- Engaging more effectively with customers across all channels of customer contact, telephone customer care, and direct marketing
- Identifying what products matched which consumers
- Getting clarity on what additional information to offer regarding home repair and maintenance
- Establishing more avenues for two-way communication with customers
- Creating opt-in-driven personalized newsletters for homeowners
- Creating a feedback portal for customers to comment on their experiences
- Establishing new protocols for escalating the most complex of claims to highly specialized teams
- Developing proactive renewal strategies that proved to homeowners that HMS was engaged and communicated the significant value of their relationship with HMS
- Developing renewal offers that matched consumer preferences

"The VOC learnings helped us develop new strategies for engaging with customers after the initial purchase decision," Doug observed. An example was the decision to connect with new customers via a relationship-oriented communication shortly after the purchase of a warranty (Figures 6.3 through 6.5).

Additionally, the renewal efforts, which had been driven largely by direct mail, were expanded to a multitouch, multichannel renewal process focused on customers' specific needs. Even though

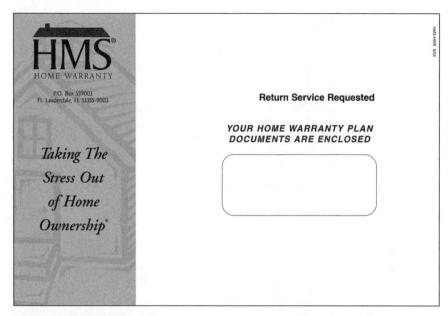

Figure 6.3: HMS National's Fulfillment Package after the VOC Research: Envelope
Source: HMS National

Figure 6.4: HMS National's Fulfillment Package after the VOC Research: First Page
Source: HMS National

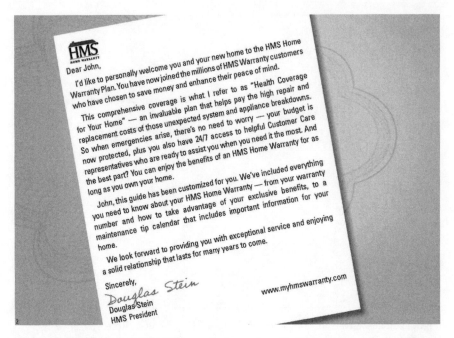

Figure 6.5: HMS National's Fulfillment Package after the VOC Research: Second Page
Source: HMS National

including new channel efforts such as telesales increased the renewal marketing expense in some segments as much as fivefold, the incremental sales more than offset the extra expense and optimized profitability.

Customer care is another essential area of HMS's business. Therefore, as an ongoing business practice at HMS, enhancements throughout customer care are planned and implemented on a regular basis. It was therefore ideal to weave specific VOC research input into the associates' enhanced training. This combination of efforts drove appreciable results as evidenced by an increase in top box satisfaction scores of 8 points. These gains materially contributed to the overall success of the renewal effort.

The VOC-informed end-to-end approach enabled a very successful customer-centric, multichannel strategy. This has driven increased renewal rates because HMS's customer experience, marketing, and offerings all came completely into alignment with customers' needs and wants.

Another Core Constituency

"The results from these efforts took our already positive results to a new level," reported Doug. "Recognizing our success with optimizing the value of our warranty and marketing to consumers, we wanted to ensure that we dedicated the same focus to our sales channel, real estate agents." To that end, HMS implemented VOC research for these business-to-business (B2B) relationships; it was a logical next step for understanding the entire sales process.

What HMS learned from the VOC interviews involving real estate professionals was invaluable. These real estate professionals outlined a "road map" for the most effective communications, sales training, and support that would enable them to be more successful in educating customers regarding the value of home warranties.

These insights helped HMS better leverage the power of this important channel. HMS was also able to use the VOC research to test potential new benefits and products for consumers. Finally, the VOC research identified how to develop an enhanced set of sales tools to win greater "top-of-mind" awareness from real estate agents and help them more effectively represent HMS.

"Based on what we learned from the VOC research with both homeowners and agents," Doug told us, "we were able to leverage the critical real estate agent first touch point with prospective buyers much more effectively." That touch point would then be followed by a redesigned, rewritten HMS welcome booklet that emphasized VOC-driven themes of consumer value, clarity, engagement, and updated benefits. The bolder, simpler new piece won praise (and increased awareness).

In addition, HMS rolled out the following VOC-driven enhancements for real estate professionals, the critical frontline sales channel:

- Providing agents with new tools and resources to help them offer HMS warranties, including key talking points and a streamlined presentation
- Creating a consistent look and feel, as well as a consistent theme of consumer value in print and online marketing materials nationwide
- Commencing proprietary, channel communications exclusively for real estate agents

- Developing a more personalized approach based on agent preference in order to strengthen the relationship between real estate agents and HMS
- Taking a more proactive approach to any agent recommendations or ideas by following up personally

The New Multichannel Strategy

This comprehensive dual-track VOC process enabled HMS to significantly expand its multichannel customer strategies quickly. The efforts were immediately recognized by both consumers and real estate professionals, and appreciable results followed.

"Consumers immediately responded to our efforts, and this was reflected in renewal rates that increased over 20 percent nationwide," Doug concluded. "As we began this initiative, HMS was looking for the right foundation from which to drive change. Ultimately, we found success by letting the change be directed by, and for, HMS's customers. Utilizing VOC research was the best way to get the information we needed to inform the change agenda. The clarity provided by the VOC process provided energy and support, direction, and details for the coalition of change we assembled. The insights from the VOC research were key to enhancing the end-to-end customer experience and achieving deeper customer engagement—and this effort is what drove our industry-leading renewal and satisfaction rates even higher."

THE CHANGING MULTICHANNEL PICTURE

We asked Bruce Biegel, senior managing director at Winterberry Group LLC, to share some thoughts on where specific marketing channels have been in recent years—and where they're going. Here's what he had to say:

> Over the past several years, we have seen a continuous shift of focus and expenditure away from the traditional marketing channels of print (that is, newspaper, magazine, catalog, and mail) to the digital channels (including search, e-mail, social, mobile, and display). This shift is equal to nearly 10

percent of the total marketing spend, and it is up from 5 percent several years ago.

The focus on digital channels for communication and commerce has accelerated through the recent downturn; yet as a percentage of spend, it is far below the 30 percent of time consumers and businesses are spending online consuming media. The question is: Why?

I believe the digital shift has been constrained by the lack of effective acquisition marketing options online. While online lead generation, data-driven display ecosystems, and search are having an impact on conversion, it is still early in the maturity cycle for influencing behavior across the entire marketing funnel in a way that drives brand engagement through to conversion.

In order for digital marketing to achieve potential equal to its share of media consumption (and thus achieve 20 to 30 percent of spend), it has to do a better job of catalyzing intent—engaging with consumers as they move down the funnel, in a way that's analogous to the way a catalog can drive a consumer to a Web site, store, or call center.

As attribution and measurement improve, allowing marketers to better understand the relationships between and across the digital channels, along with the relationship to the offline channels, we expect to see a greater understanding of the right media mix to achieve marketing objectives. Part of this process is the shift toward targeting specific audiences across the Web instead of buying content to reach an audience. We are evolving targeting and optimization platforms that show the right offers to the right people at the right time. I believe that these platforms will mature and make the Web experience better for consumers and for marketers, thus driving spend increases online over the next several years, and continuing the pattern of taking share from traditional media.

Up: Search, display, e-mail, mobile, social, addressable TV, digital out-of-home media

Down: Mail, newspaper, magazine (offline)

Neutral: Radio and TV

NOW WHAT?

- Identify innovative multichannel initiatives that engage customers in new ways and across many parts of their life cycle and lifestyle. Nike offers several creative strategies.
- Place more importance on being interested than on being interesting.
- Engage locally. This is the only reliable way to beat worldwide brands.
- Individualize multichannel communication with consumers and key allies.
- Consider creating alliances with key players in the support network of your consumers (such as midwives and doctors in the case of new parents, or real estate agents in the case of home buyers). These relationships may create new, competitively differentiating channels for you.
- Build a multichannel strategy that supports your opt-in strategy. Collect only the information that will be used to drive relevant and personally useful information and/or resources to customers.

In the next part of the book, you'll find out how to use everything you've learned up to this point to create social media strategies that deepen customer engagement and increase lifetime value and word-of-mouth recommendations.

CREATE A VOC-DRIVEN SOCIAL MEDIA PRESENCE

SERVICE

OPT-IN

VOICE OF CUSTOMER

SOCIAL MEDIA
(Step 4)

MULTICHANNEL

HARNESSING THE POWER OF VOC-DRIVEN SOCIAL MEDIA

EXECUTIVE SUMMARY

- Today, success in marketing is achieved as the result of a series of personal "conversations" and points of engagement with consumers and prospects.
- Ford Motor Company designed a social media–driven plan to create such engagements. Results were remarkable: 4.5 million YouTube views, 3.5 million Twitter impressions, and 80,000 "hand raisers" who asked to be kept up to date on the U.S. launch of the Ford Fiesta. Of all those hand raisers, *97 percent* did not own a Ford vehicle.
- Such numbers are the result of an unprecedented relationship engagement initiative at Ford.
- Social media tools represent not a means for "selling" but a means for creating or improving relationships with consumers.
- Selling becomes a by-product of the quality and mutual benefit of those relationships.

The act of connecting with others virtually, via online social media, is now part of our daily life. This dimension of remote connection with others has taken, and will continue to take, many forms. The vehicles for these remote connections will continue to change at an astonishing pace, but the underlying requirement to engage with customers at high levels of relevance and value will remain.

Whatever the future holds for marketers, we believe that social media—best understood not as a single platform but as a constantly shifting mix of interactive portals—represent an opportunity for a new "gold standard" in marketing. In the twenty-first century, success in marketing is achieved as the result of a series of personal engagements with consumers and prospects.

In this chapter, you'll learn the requirements for success through Ford Motor Company's story, which shows how a company that's over a century old has reinvented itself via unorthodox, creative, and effective use of social media.

If you are trying to communicate, as we are, that you have been reinventing the company, you can't just say it. You have to get the people to say it to each other.
                                    —JAMES FARLEY, CHIEF MARKETING EXECUTIVE,
                                                    FORD MOTOR COMPANY

Social media marketing makes use of social networks, blogs, online communities, and other online collaborative media to support the interrelated functions of marketing, sales, public relations, and customer service. As of this writing, important social media marketing tools include Twitter, LinkedIn, Facebook, Flickr, and YouTube.

Typically, social media channels feature content primarily published by users, not by employees of the owners of the channel. (For instance, most content on Facebook is not published by employees of Facebook.)

CONVERSATION, CONNECTION, INTERACTION

To be sure, there has always been the potential for engagement with customers and prospects on the Internet, but the meteoric rise of social media has placed a new emphasis on classic marketing principles of *conversation, connection, and ongoing interaction*. The critical difference between now and years past, as we have seen, is that the prospect or consumer is clearly in control of the conversation, the means of connection, and the decisions concerning how, or whether, to continue interactions.

Thus, these media represent not a means for "selling" but a means for creating or improving relationships. Selling becomes a by-product of the quality and mutual benefit of those relationships.

That point may seem obvious to master salespeople, and to readers like you who have followed us this far in this book, but the fact remains that most social media experiences with marketing organizations fail the test demanded by today's consumers: the test of relevance.

THE TEST OF RELEVANCE

Consumers—now used to engaging with whomever they want, whenever they choose, via whatever channel they choose—conduct a series of ongoing tests that make conversation, connection, and ongoing interaction possible with certain parties, and not with others. This test of relevance, which occurs so frequently that it is now a constant factor, marks the threshold at which prospects and customers decide whether someone merits continued attention and engagement. If we pass this relevance test, we will be allowed into the individual consumer's world, perhaps as a trusted resource. If we fail the test, we will be shut out.

More and more, consumers are conducting this test by means of social media, and they are ruthlessly eliminating relationships with marketers who fail the test.

A CRITICAL MIGRATION TO FACEBOOK

According to Free The Children founder Craig Kielburger, one sign of the influence of Facebook is the remarkable stability of its profiles within a notoriously change-happy user group: children and teenagers. More and more of these young users, according to Kielburger, are using Facebook as their "home base," relying on the site much more heavily than on traditional e-mail accounts and holding on to a single profile there over time.

That trend stands in stark contrast to profiles in accounts set up in other communication platforms, where young people are far more likely to open up multiple profiles or abandon profiles altogether without warning.

Kielburger believes the difference is attributable to the amount of time and effort that goes into establishing a Facebook profile, and the high relevance of the many relationships that connect to that profile. The migration to Facebook carries immense implications to marketers because the young people in question have decades of purchasing decisions ahead of them.

You'll hear more from Craig in Chapter 9.

FOUR UNMISTAKABLE ATTRIBUTES OF THE SOCIAL MEDIA MARKETING ENVIRONMENT

Most people already know that the social media marketing environment offers these three unmistakable attributes:

Power: Whole new markets emerge in the blink of an eye in today's socially connected world; by the same token, many old-line industries are presented with the choice of rapid adaptation or extinction.

Speed: Whereas consumer results and responses were once measured in days, months, and weeks, they are now measured in hours, minutes, and seconds.

Volatility: Sudden, rapid, and unpredictable change is the order of the day. Major players like Netscape may vanish; seemingly indispensable communication tools like Facebook and YouTube materialize—and dominate popular culture—in ways both sudden and impossible to forecast.

A fourth unmistakable attribute, however, often goes unnoticed: *engagement.*

ENGAGEMENT

The marketing initiative that thrives in today's connected environment is one that permits, supports, and encourages engagement with the consumer.

Consider the research from McKinsey & Company, for instance, that found that people who participate in an effective online community return to a site *nine times as often* and *five times as long as people who don't!* This represents a 45-fold increase in loyalty—an outcome that would seem to settle, once and for all, the question of whether social media carry a bottom-line benefit.

Only if we engage with people will we be perceived as relevant in their world, and today, we have no choice but to engage with them online.

Marketers who use social media as a tool for ongoing engagement with prospects and customers, and who actually listen to those prospects and customers, will benefit in two ways. The first is a loyal base of customers who are willing and eager to sing the praises of the organization. The second is a willingness on the part of consumers to provide (brutally) honest feedback regarding areas for improvement and give the organization a second chance in the event that something goes wrong. Both are essential to the ongoing success of a corporation.

It's important to emphasize here that we cannot "fake" engagement with customers or prospects. We are either relevant to their world, and worthy of inclusion within it, or we are not.

No one man can, for any considerable time, wear one face to himself, and another to the multitude, without finally getting bewildered as to which is the true one.
—NATHANIEL HAWTHORNE

THE ONLINE DISCONNECT

In spite of the benefits we've just discussed, results from hundreds of VOC interviews we have conducted indicate that customers and prospects are consistently disappointed by their virtual experiences with companies.

Reasons for this dissatisfaction include these:

- Frustration that they cannot truly *"connect"* with the company online due to the *impersonal, transactional, or generic nature of the experience.* This feeling of "disconnection" from a company carries potentially disastrous implications in an era when competitors can quickly and inexpensively establish relationships with large groups of people using social media marketing.

- Perception that communications are not relevant or authentic, despite many opportunities to capture or use behavioral and transactional information to drive relevant communications.
- Disappointment that the expected company "brand experience" is missing from the online experience, thus creating an uncomfortable disconnect. This is a lack of authenticity. Consumers have been led to believe they will experience one thing, via ads or other communications, and they are disappointed to find only transactional experiences online. Very often, there is a lack of meaningful personalization in communications, which further fuels alienation and feelings of irrelevance.
- Expectation that online experiences will allow for opt-in profiling to indicate their preferences, so future interactions and communications will be more relevant and targeted. If opt-in profiling is offered, the company's follow-up communications and offers often do not reflect those expressed preferences.
- Lack of a sense of community among fellow shoppers, visitors, or customers.

This "community" requirement is important, and it plays out in complex ways. This theme has come up repeatedly, across multiple industries, in many of the VOC Relationship Research efforts we've conducted. The common themes across these research efforts are striking.

It's as though the prospective buyer were saying: "Use your Internet presence to help me connect at three levels: with peers who have interests and needs similar to the ones I have; with experts who can provide me with detailed information; and, last, with your company."

CASE STUDY:
FORD REINVENTS ITSELF AND LEVERAGES SOCIAL MEDIA

CLOSE-UP ON FORD MOTOR COMPANY
- Founded in 1903
- Headquarters: Dearborn, Michigan

- Multinational automaker
- Over 200,000 employees worldwide
- www.ford.com

Of the three major American auto manufacturers who faced major market challenges in 2008 and 2009, it was Ford who emerged from the waves of negative publicity, recession-driven buying slowdowns, unpleasant public hearings in Washington, and consumer skepticism. Ford came out of the deluge with its reputation, and its prospects for future growth, intact.

Different industry analysts have offered many explanations as to why Ford was able to turn things around, but we think the answer has to do with three factors: the quality of the company's vehicles, its innovative strategy for engagement with the consumer, and its compelling demonstration of relevance to the consumer's world.

Relevance was a central theme in Ford's traditional broadcast media, which featured actual consumers talking about their own experiences in Ford vehicles. No actors, no paid PR people, no "beauty shots" of vehicles performing unlikely maneuvers—just real Ford owners sharing honest emotions about their vehicles, which they clearly loved. It was quite effective.

If you only watched TV, though, you missed the most impressive, and perhaps the most critical, part of Ford's marketing initiative in the crucial 2008 to 2009 period, which was its social media campaign. In 2009, Ford spent roughly one-quarter of its marketing dollars on digital and social media. This was more than double the amount spent by its competitors. Ford was clearly out front in the social networking arena, and its efforts paid rich dividends. As Ford's chief marketing executive, James Farley, put it: "If you are trying to communicate, as we are, that you have been reinventing the company, you can't just say it. *You have to get the people to say it to each other.*"

Say it they did! They posted 11,000 videos, 15,000 Twitter messages, and over 11 million social networking impressions as part of an American Ford Fiesta prelaunch social media campaign called the Fiesta Movement.

FORD'S FIESTA MOVEMENT SCORECARD

- 4.5 million YouTube views
- 3.5 million Twitter impressions
- 80,000 "hand raisers" who asked to be kept up to date on the U.S. launch of the Fiesta, *97 percent of whom did not own a Ford vehicle*
- 1,000 people who reserved a Fiesta online (informally, with no purchase commitment)
- 37 percent Fiesta brand awareness among Generation Y members, roughly equal to the awareness levels of the traditionally promoted Fusion and Flex models

The Fiesta Movement was born in support of the Ford Fiesta, a vehicle that was not yet even available in the United States. Yet somehow the car became an Internet sensation among American car buyers: Ford's YouTube presence easily outshone that of rival carmakers, auto industry writers began to pick up the buzz, and 80,000 prospects told Ford they wanted to be kept up to date regarding when, where, and how the car would finally become available for purchase in the U.S. market.

How did Ford pull it off? By building a great car, of course. What happened after that, though, was what drew the most notice among marketers. Ford gave—you read it right, gave—100 Fiestas to 100 American drivers in 2008, a year and a half before the car was to materialize in auto showrooms. The 100 independent real-world users/bloggers posted enthusiastic videos, blog entries, and Facebook exchanges about what it was like to drive the Fiesta; the program was paralleled by a similar real-folks-driving-real-cars video offering inspiring dialogue about the Ford brand as a whole at FordStory.com.

The bottom line: People responded. Ford had engaged directly with consumers, and it had done so in a way that was (judging by the tone of the YouTube videos) deeply relevant to their world.

Before 2008, a major promotional campaign launched 18 months before the product was actually available to consumers was a bit of an anomaly in the auto industry—or perhaps in any industry. Why promote a car that consumers couldn't yet buy? Yet the Fiesta Movement worked. Gary Dilts, senior vice president of J.D. Power's automotive practice, had this to say about the Fiesta Movement program: "I think the Fiesta campaign, and the other digital video Ford is running, is already a case study for any marketer in or out of the auto industry."

A LONG WAY FROM THE DARK DAYS OF 2008

Magna International (NYSE: MGA) shares dropped sharply today after billionaire Kirk Kerkorian announced he may sell his entire stake in Ford Motors (NYSE: F). . . . The move puts further pressure on Ford and other U.S. automakers that have been struggling to get by amid the most difficult market since the Great Depression.

—Investerms, October 21, 2008

If January 2010 was a homerun for Ford sales (and it was), . . . then February knocked it completely out of the ballpark. Ford, Lincoln, and Mercury sales for February 2010 were up 43 percent versus a year ago and 22 percent higher than January. "The strength of our new products and Ford's leadership in quality, fuel efficiency, safety, smart design, and value are resonating with customers," said Ken Czubay, Ford Vice President, U.S. Marketing Sales and Service. . . . February sales were higher throughout Ford's line-up. Cars were up 54 percent versus a year ago, utilities were up 39 percent, and trucks were up 36 percent. Among brands, Ford sales were up 46 percent, Lincoln sales were up 19 percent, and Mercury sales were up 24 percent.

—FordStory.com

Ford's use of social media contributed to a major consumer reassessment of the Ford brand.

We spoke at length with the person who engineered Ford's social media marketing efforts, Scott Monty, global digital and multimedia communications manager. Following are some important takeaways from the conversation:

ERNAN ROMAN (ER): You've brought engagement with the automotive consumer to a whole new level through innovative campaigns using social media like YouTube and Twitter. As the person responsible for spearheading the Ford social media campaigns, how would you describe the major objectives of those campaigns?

SCOTT MONTY (SM): I think overall, one of the things we've been trying to do at every level within the company is to demonstrate the fact that Ford really is different. Now, the way we convey that is important because *people inherently don't trust what companies say about themselves.* They trust what people like them say, and they trust what third-party experts say, but they don't really trust what the companies themselves have to say about what they're doing and what they've accomplished. So the notion that we can continue to work with third-party experts and independent media, and do that in a way that wins people's attention outside of the world of automotive journalists, is critical for us.

By the same token, the more we can engage with consumers directly for their input, their feedback, and their experiences with Ford vehicles, the better off we are. What we find too is that the more directly and personally we engage with consumers, the more authentic and the more believable the messages we get from them turn out to be.

ER: How do you explain the strength of the online response to your message?

SM: *Well, it's not just our message.* It's a conversation. Pretty much since the dawn of the automotive industry, everyone has had a car story to tell. Whatever it happens to be, everyone has some kind of a car story, and what we acknowledged was that most people really like telling that story to someone. Now, these conversations have traditionally taken place in neighborhood bars, or in supermarkets, or over the backyard fence. Of course, that will continue to happen; that's just human nature, because we are, by nature, storytellers. We've been telling stories since the days when the first communities gathered around a fire and listened to what happened during the hunt. Today, though, a lot of those conversations are happening online. And that's an important shift because that medium of story-telling gives us as a company the opportunity to listen in. We can tell what people are saying and how they're talking about us and our vehicles. It also gives us an unparalleled opportunity to jump into those conversations and provide some input—maybe educate, maybe dispel some inaccuracies, maybe engage in order to get feedback that will help us to improve our next round of vehicles.

It's not just our message. It's a conversation.
—SCOTT MONTY, GLOBAL DIGITAL & MULTIMEDIA COMMUNICATIONS
MANAGER, FORD MOTOR COMPANY

ER: As of this writing, Ford has experienced greater success in the marketplace than some of its competitors, despite a global economic downturn. Do you think Ford's social media initiatives have had something to do with that?

SM: Yes. Ultimately, if, in the process of doing all that communicating, we're exposing the people behind the blue oval, the people behind the Ford logo, that's good because that's what the public wants. People don't want to have a conversation with a brand. They want to talk to another real human being. They want to talk to other people who can understand their concerns, people who can empathize with them, who can laugh with them. And as we continue to push forward in humanizing Ford Motor Company, we'll be connecting our employees with our constituents, and providing value along the way. That's the essential underpinning to everything that we do in social media: that humanization of the company. And it doesn't come only through the humanization of our employees; it also comes through the humanization of our advocates—whether they're dealers or other vehicle owners or whatever. We're allowing people to connect with other members of the public who can help to amplify the Ford story. When we put like-minded people together with social media, that helps us tell our story and also helps make the relationship with our customers—and our prospective customers—an active relationship.

The Takeaways:
Ford—The Five Best Practices for Achieving Engagement and Relevance with Social Media

Best practice 1. Forget about the hard sell.

The aim is to create a *relationship* that will enable customers and prospects to tell you what is relevant to them, what they want to see next, what's working, and what isn't.

Scott Monty is as eager to track down ideas for design improvements on Ford vehicles as he is to generate success stories. This willingness to listen is the critical starting point for an effective social media initiative. If there is no willingness to listen, there is no engagement and little possibility of establishing relevance in the buyers' world. If you were at a party with some close friends, and a salesman in a bad plaid suit burst in the door, handed out business cards to everyone in sight, drained down a couple of glasses of punch, and then vanished—how eager would you be to seek out the salesman and learn more about what he had to offer?

Best practice 2. Personalize, personalize, personalize.

Today, people are looking for points of commonality and points of connection with those they allow into their circle. That's why it's a good idea to share appropriate personal insights and experiences; to the degree possible, you should try to establish an independent, credible viewpoint for what you share with the world. Don't be afraid to share a little attitude now and then. When Ford executives were testifying before Congress, Scott Monty sent the following message about Ford CEO Alan Mulally to everyone following him on Twitter: "I told Alan that if things turn nasty in DC, he should take the Mustang and do donuts on the Capitol lawn."

THE PERSONALIZATION OF THE GLOBAL MARKETPLACE CONTINUES: IS THAT STEVE JOBS IN YOUR INBOX?

A recent *New York Times* article ("Ding! Mail. OMG! It's Steve Jobs," March 24, 2010) reported that the once-reclusive Apple

Computer leader was igniting a firestorm of interest on the Internet—and quickly resolving problems—by taking a personalized approach to customer complaints. The *Times* reported that Jobs's personal e-mail replies to customer inquiries to Apple had apparently become much more common. The media coverage—and the waves in the blogosphere—proved once again that we live in an age when marketing, promotion, and customer service are sometimes indistinguishable.

Best practice 3. Synchronize PR and social media.

This means updating classic vehicles such as press releases and brochures to include easy-to-access information on how to engage in a dialogue with the company via Facebook, Twitter, or other channels. It also means revising the classic "interruptive" marketing model to one that's more in tune with PR's traditional skill at engaging members of "the media" in conversations about a given topic. The only difference now is that anyone who's connected to social media is, by definition, a member of "the media"! Speaking with one coordinated voice to the people who can help you spread your message—whether they are writing a column for the *New York Times* or updating their personal status on Facebook—is now a strategic and marketplace advantage.

Best practice 4. Target effectively, and respond quickly to everyone you target.

Once you know who your target customer or prospect is, you must find a way to create prompt responses for that customer or prospect. Even if you don't have the solution to a Twitter-launched complaint, get back to the person, apologize for the difficulty the person is experiencing, and say you're working on the problem. Then work on the problem!

Very often, customers and prospects use social media channels to test whether someone is actually listening. Proving that you *are* listening is one of the best ways to differentiate your organization from competitors who are stuck in an old-fashioned, unresponsive mode.

Similarly, members of the media now use social media to test an organization's responsiveness and ability to follow through on commitments. Today, a consumer's response time expectation is likely to be measured in minutes. If you have to change your staffing arrangements in order to come closer to meeting that expectation, you should consider doing so. Remember, when a complaint goes unaddressed online, lots of people notice—not just the person who complained.

Best practice 5. Tell a story.

The power of the right narrative, when shared in a powerful and compelling way, is hard to overstate. Case in point: Ford's response to the public outcry that followed its executives' 2008 appearance on Capitol Hill. The coverage of the hearings had the potential to leave a major misimpression: that Ford was looking for a big infusion of federal dollars as part of an emergency bailout arrangement. (It wasn't.)

As Scott Monty wrote in a blog posting, "In a massive flurry of activity and cross-departmental coordination, in the five days over Thanksgiving weekend, we created The Ford Story. It was a huge win for us, as it demonstrated the One Ford mission that drives the company, and it got a lot of coverage and attention for its design and good content. We wanted to ensure that we were true to our strategy, so we led with faces on every page: our executives speaking unscripted and plainly . . . about what Ford stood for." This site—which told the story "Ford Has Successfully Reinvented Itself"—continues to get positive responses from consumers, bloggers, and members of the traditional media.

BY THE NUMBERS: SOCIAL MEDIA ARE HERE TO STAY

As if any further proof were needed, the following statistics offer some sense of the massive size of the social media wave. That wave is growing by the hour. The choice for marketers is a clear one: Will we ride the wave? Or be swept away by it?

- Number of hours of video uploaded every hour onto YouTube, according to the YouTube blog: 20

- Number of new Facebook members added per day, according to Inside Facebook: 600,000
- Number of tweets sent daily on Twitter, according to TechCrunch: 4 million
- Number of U.S. mobile social network subscribers, according to Informa Global Markets (IGM): 92.5 million

WHAT ABOUT EMPLOYEES WHO USE SOCIAL MEDIA TO "WASTE TIME"?

To those who worry about the potential downside of giving employees access to social media tools during work hours, Ford's Scott Monty offers the following cautionary tale:

A while back, there was a major corporation whose employees wanted to start using some of the new, cutting-edge communications technology during work hours. The employees said they wanted to make this change because they wanted to do a better job of keeping in touch with customers, vendors, and employees in remote locations. This request puzzled members of the senior management team, who were used to doing things the way things had always been done on their watch. The company's most experienced leaders were afraid that giving the team permission to use this new medium in the office—while people were actually on the clock!—would lead to excess socializing, irresponsible use of company resources, and unacceptable drops in productivity.

The employees persisted, however, and after months of requests, management eventually agreed to a trial period. This trial would be part of a larger study to determine whether the new communications media represented a net gain or a net loss from the company's perspective.

After the trial period concluded, the study results were announced: Employees were in fact significantly more productive when they were allowed to reach out to others using the latest technology. What's more, customers were significantly more likely to buy, and more likely to become long-term customers, when employees used the new communications tools to initiate and maintain contact.

Here's the kicker: The year of the study was 1930. And the "new communications tool" was the telephone.

We share that story here to make three important points about multichannel marketing. First and foremost, we handicap our employees when we deny them the tools our competitors are using. Second, the media mix by which Americans have been receiving marketing messages, and acting on those marketing messages, has been evolving since at least the days of Benjamin Franklin, who launched the world's first mail order catalog in the 1700s. And third, we can expect the social media mix to continue to evolve in ways we cannot imagine. The biggest organizational sin when it comes to adapting to social media is going to be denial.

NOW WHAT?

- Build loyalty through *engagement*. People who participate in an effective online community return to a site nine times as often and five times as long as people who don't.
- Try to weed out the impersonal, transactional, or generic customer experiences so they don't cause customers or prospects to feel that they cannot connect with your organization, express preferences, and experience the promised brand experience.
- Harness the power of narrative. Tell a story about your organization or someone connected to it.
- Forget about the hard sell. Focus instead on connection and conversation.
- Personalize, personalize, personalize. Strive to provide prospects and customers information and resources that are directly relevant to their lives.

- Synchronize PR and social media. Send the same core message through all channels ("Ford Has Successfully Reinvented Itself," for example).
- Target effectively, and respond quickly to everyone you target. Once you identify your customer, the relationship is precious. Follow through promptly on the conversation with that person—and remember that social media networking has turned customer response time expectations into minutes and hours, not days or weeks.
- Give your people access to the social media tools they need to do the job.

If you believe VOC-driven social media networking is only for big operations like Ford, read on. The next chapter will prove that adopting it is a matter of survival for organizations of all sizes.

CHAPTER

8

GUIDELINES FOR USING VOC-DRIVEN SOCIAL MEDIA TO ENGAGE THE NEW CONSUMER

EXECUTIVE SUMMARY

- The days of ignoring social media feedback about what your organization is doing are over.
- A successful social media strategy demands engagement, personalization, and effective targeting.
- Engagement led Threadless to 30 percent margins.
- Personalization allowed IBM to reposition itself with a critical target market of decision makers, generating a return visitor rate of 65 percent and a weekly rate of growth in the community of 10 percent.
- Sophisticated targeting using Google Ads has enabled the online customized stationery store Tiny Prints to turn profits since the year it was founded, 2004.

Have you noticed a change in the online weather? Back in the long-ago and far-away days of, say, 2005, when a marketing initiative didn't work, consumers could generally be counted on to keep their mouths shut about it. Oh, a few industry insiders might notice a problem with a misguided campaign—or perhaps, once in a great while, an ad would be so offensive as to attract the interest of someone in the mainstream media. But by and large, open consumer revolts against bad advertising ideas were not something people in marketing had to plan for.

McNeil Consumer Healthcare, the maker of Motrin, now knows better. In the fall of 2008, the company launched a bizarre online video advertisement about moms who wore baby slings. The copy read this way:

> Wearing your baby seems to be in fashion. I mean, in theory it's a great idea. There's the front baby carrier, sling, schwing, wrap, pouch. And who knows what else they've come up with. Wear your baby on your side, your front, go hands free. Supposedly, it's a real bonding experience. They say that babies carried close to the body tend to cry less than others. But what about me? Do moms that wear their babies cry more than those who don't? I sure do! These things put a ton of strain on your back, your neck, your shoulders. Did I mention your back? I mean, I'll put up with the pain because it's a good kind of pain; it's for my kid. Plus, it totally makes me look like an official mom. And so if I look tired and crazy, people will understand why.

Moms took exception to the notion that they wore the slings to be fashionable; they also weren't happy about being labeled as "crazy" as a result of wearing them. Many of them took the ad as a parody of baby-sling-wearers.

The ad didn't just not work—it launched an avalanche of criticism from disgruntled moms via Twitter, YouTube, and various blog postings.

A phone interview with the ad agency that created the campaign made it clear that no one at the agency, or at McNeil, had been paying attention to the mounting wave of online rage—a fact that only fueled the sense of alienation and disconnect from the people being targeted.

Indeed, Motrin was (by modern standards) slow to respond to the problem, and it appears to have believed that pulling the ad and posting an apology would be enough. A few years earlier, that might have made the problem go away. This time around, though, consumers took

McNeil's failure to engage with them *via the social media channels they were using* as a further sign of the company's cluelessness. The clumsy, delayed response meant the company was not part of "us." As one tweet put it:

> note to self . . . never piss off moms . . . especially twitter moms . . . they can be a nasty bunch ;)

The moral: Using social media to engage with your customers and get their ongoing feedback about what you're doing isn't a nice "add-on" for you to do if you have the time. It's a survival measure. Failing to do it may leave you facing a "nasty bunch" of your own making!

In this chapter, you will see how three companies—information technology giant IBM, apparel designer Threadless, and online greeting card retailer Tiny Prints—have taken a proactive approach to online engagement, an approach based on dialogue, personalization, and effective targeting via social media.

CASE STUDY:
THE THREADLESS REVOLUTION

CLOSE-UP ON THREADLESS
- Founded 2000
- Headquarters: Chicago, Illinois
- Community-centered online apparel store specializing in T-shirts designed by members of the community
- Approximately 80 employees
- www.threadless.com

Let's assume marketers want to sell T-shirts online. How should they go about doing it? If you were to ask a handful of T-shirt retailers that question, you might hear answers like these:

- Buy humorous ads that appeal to people in your target demo-graphic; get people to click on your ad in order to get the answer to a puzzle or download a special ringtone for their cell phone; then ask for their e-mail address before you give them what they're after. Once you've got that e-mail address, send them wave after wave of advertisements about T-shirts.
- Track down all the sites where people buy online apparel, and then pay for eye-catching banner ads so you can win clicks from those customers, and eventually lure them away from the competition.
- Give free T-shirts away to everyone who visits your Web site; pub-licize the initiative through a wacky PR campaign at a local sports arena that involves using a slingshot to hurl shirts into the hands of fans.

As common as these approaches might be—and they are indeed common—you've perhaps guessed that they are not exactly driven by VOC marketing. For an example of a company that takes the VOC approach to a whole new level, and implements Scott Monty's advice to abandon the hard sell and focus on relationships, we offer Threadless: a community-driven online apparel retailer headquartered in Chicago. Threadless has used customer interaction and feedback to create a whole new kind of enterprise.

Not Your Average T-shirt Company

We are not your average tee shirt company. The art for our tees is sourced from our ongoing open call for tee shirt submissions from a worldwide community of amazing artists and designers. Once sub-mitted, our community of over 1 million registered users cast their votes, which helps us decide which designs become Threadless tee shirts. In 2008 alone, we awarded over $1 million to artists around the world for their work—young and old, professional and amateur alike.

—Threadless.com

Threadless is built on a simple, revolutionary premise: customers come up with good ideas, and these ideas can drive product development and marketing.

Back in November 2000, founders Jake Nickell and Jacob DeHart held a contest, asking designers who were part of an online forum called Dreamless.org to submit their own T-shirt designs. The prize for designing one of the top two shirts was distinctly low rent: two copies of the finished T-shirt and a commitment that proceeds from the sales of the garments would fund future such contests. Nickell and DeHart got less than 100 submissions (some of which had unlikely titles like "Dead Sexy Designer"). "We let the money build up slowly, and when we had enough to print another design, we did," Nickell recalled. Soon, he and DeHart had implemented a sophisticated online process for letting community members offer input to the contests, and they upgraded the prize award to include cash payments.

Nowadays, the up-front prize money for the comparatively small number of winning shirts at Threadless is $2,000 and a $500 gift certificate. A decade or so after the company's founding, though, cash awards still aren't the main reason undiscovered designers post their designs for evaluation and critique by the huge Threadless.com community. Aspiring designers keep logging on to post their designs at Threadless for a single, impossible-to-forget reason: to get discovered.

The Customer-Driven Company

Threadless's breakthrough social networking formula is based on the principle that people from the community can generate both the core product and the best voice of customer marketing guidance. Users drive the business. They log in to post new T-shirt designs; they take special pride in spotting the coolest of the bunch; they help reward the best designers with recognition and remuneration from the company. They also purchase the resulting apparel at $9 a shirt and up— and they do so in very large numbers. Hundreds of new shirt designs are posted, and rated, every week; thousands of backorder items are available through the Threadless online store or at one of its two retail outlets.

The three core groups that make up the extremely active Threadless online community—designers, reviewers, and purchasers—often overlap. True to its own promise, Threadless gives them all an experience that is nothing like a traditional apparel company. For instance: the company doesn't rely on traditional advertising to sell the elite group of shirts that end up making the grade. Instead, it lets its community members do the advertising . . . and the buying. Crazy homemade titles for the shirts are still part of the mix: one recent, elaborately illustrated entry boasted the name "The Cat Who Mistook His Wife (and the Kids, and the Furniture and Even the Parrot) for a Hat." Another text-only shirt promised boldly, "I Listen to Bands That Don't Even Exist Yet."

There are plenty of differences from management's side as well, including competitive advantages that most apparel vendors only dream of. R&D expenses are low. Profit margins are high—*Inc.* magazine said that Threadless's margins were over 30 percent in 2005. According to Nickell, the risk involved in printing new designs is "quite small." The company does not accept preorders—only customer votes and signals of intent to buy.

Thus, the company's business model doesn't require the company to invest in production or inventory costs until *after* community members have helped executives determine which products are likely to be profitable. This guarantees Threadless a nearly risk-free launch, shirt after shirt after shirt. A more powerful vindication of the VOC marketing model is hard to imagine.

The key to this revolutionary model: an emphasis on engagement over sales pitches. A study conducted by *Sloan Management Review* found that 95 percent of those purchasing shirts at Threadless.com have voted and posted comments on some of the community's designs before making a purchase. Translation: virtually everyone participates in the discussion, and hardly anyone logs on just to buy a shirt. There's a catch, though: Threadless has to keep listening to the community. So far, there have been no signs of disconnect. Direct engagement with even the senior-most company officials is part of the culture.

Today, Nickell is Threadless's chief strategy officer; DeHart has moved on to new business ventures. The impact of the two Threadless founders' participatory, community-driven vision back in 2000 is still sending shock waves through the apparel industry (and, for that matter, just about every other industry). Whether you refer to what Threadless has accomplished as "crowdsourcing," "open-source marketing," or "user-centered innovation"—and it's been written up using all three names—the company has proven that it's possible not only to build a company around customers but also to use what you learn from customers to drive both sales and innovation.

We asked Threadless CEO Thomas Ryan to share some thoughts on his company's social media revolution, as witnessed from the inside:

ERNAN ROMAN (ER): Why do people who log on get so excited about Threadless.com?

THOMAS RYAN (TR): Artists get excited by submitting their designs to Threadless for several reasons. Of course, there is the general excitement that comes with entering a challenge as well as the prospect of winning that challenge. The recognition is an important motivator, since it's fulfilling to have the quality of one's work acknowledged by peers. In fact, winning a Threadless design challenge has become a recognized portfolio piece among graphic designers, and it is something that gets shown to prospective clients and employers. However, the cash compensation is significant—$2,000 in cash plus $500 in Threadless credit for the initial design, plus the potential to earn more from reprint fees and for winning recognition for creating the best design of the month or the year. Each year, one talented designer who is awarded the Bestee of the Year makes $25,000 from a single design.

All the same, you don't need to win to get a lot of value out of Threadless. Joining a community of like-minded artists and getting valuable feedback on your designs so you can develop your skills as an artist are also major motivators. Clearly, given that hundreds of designs are submitted for each one that is printed, artists don't need to win to value the entire process greatly.

Participants enjoy Threadless for a variety of reasons, but it all stems from being part of an active, vibrant community. And you don't need to be an artist to be a prominent, respected member of the community. Many participants enjoy voting on designs and having a say in which designs ultimately become Threadless products. Lots of them enjoy reading and interacting on our active blogs section, where myriad topics related to art, Threadless, and other issues are discussed. In fact, one of our members has made a part-time job of doing extensive blog interviews of all the employees here at Threadless. And then there are the quiet members of the community. Some folks just like to lurk.

Customers love the fresh new designs that we release each week. They know there is always something new and that they can't find these designs elsewhere. They also like that the designs and the design selection is the result of a community effort. We believe the diversity and quality of the designs we print are unrivaled, and millions of customers and fans seem to agree!

ER: Is there a story you can share with us about a particularly successful product that would have been impossible without the kind of community engagement you have created at Threadless?

TR: The one that comes to mind is a project that took advantage of our ability to get early and direct access to what the whole Threadless community was thinking about, spot trends early, and move very quickly. In this case, we were able to launch a new product that was based on two huge viral Internet events that had already peaked in 2009, combine them, and create a third event.

The first of these events was a humorous YouTube video called "Keyboard Cat" that showed a cat playing the piano; to date it has scored over 5 million views. The other was a T-shirt called "Three Wolf Moon" that had become something of a camp phenomenon on Amazon.com—it's a shirt that shows a trio of wolves howling at the moon. This wasn't one of our shirts, but it was already legendary as a viral joke, and people had posted plenty of snarky comments on Amazon.com making fun of the shirt's supposed ability to attract members of the opposite sex. What we did was create a parody shirt that fused the two designs and created a third viral joke: instead of three reverently posed wolves, we showed three reverently posed cats playing keyboards. It was basically an in-joke for people who had been in on the other two jokes. We called it "Three Keyboard Cat Moon." And, thanks to the humorous postings of a lot of our community members on sites like Digg.com, the shirt started an Internet wave; it was just off the charts in terms of total votes on Threadless. In fact, it set a new record for us.

The thing about Internet waves, though, is that you have to act quickly in order to make the most of them. After just one day, we realized that we had a winner, so we put the shirt into production. That whole week, we were able to capitalize on the wave. So, if you stop to think about all the ways our own customers were able to point us in the right direction on that project, you'll see that what we were able to accomplish was really totally community driven. Our designers were part of the community that made the "mashup" design in the first place; not only did our customers prove that the design was viable commercially but they also served as critical components of the online "buzz" that drove the marketing. In the span of a week or two, the product really took off and won a lot of attention. We were able to use community validation and information to put the right resources to work, and capture all the potential of an intense, but very short, viral cycle of interest on the Internet. Once it became hot, it seemed like everyone wanted one of those shirts, and we had many, many people coming in to help with production. Capitalizing on that short-term interest was possible only because of the virtuous circle of users who knew what we were parodying, loved it, confirmed its viability, and helped us to spread the word.

The Takeaways

ER: What advice would you share with someone trying to replicate your success, and your community focus, in another industry?

TR: Make sure that you and your core team understand and are representative of the online community you're creating. Authenticity is nonnegotiable. Understanding the subtleties of what makes a given community tick is essential, and it's something best done by someone who is actually from that world.

> **BY THE NUMBERS:**
> **THE THREADLESS REVOLUTION**
>
> Total users: Over 1 million (source: Threadless.com)
> Annual sales (estimated): $30 million (source: *Inc.* magazine)
> Margin (estimated): 30 percent (source: *Inc.* magazine)

CASE STUDY: IBM

CLOSE-UP ON IBM
- Headquarters: Armonk, New York
- Global multinational computer, technology, and IT consulting corporation
- Approximately 400,000 employees worldwide
- www.ibm.com

At its heart, social networking is all about making connections at a fundamental, human level.

—LESLIE REISER, INTERACTIVE MARKETING
PROGRAM DIRECTOR, IBM

Personalize, Personalize, Personalize:
IBM and the InfoBOOM!

One of the world's most admired brands, multinational company and information technology (IT) consulting giant IBM, has faced some unique challenges within the critical midmarket. These challenges resulted from a number of factors, including access, awareness of IBM's vast portfolio of midmarket solutions and services, and how they apply to clients and prospects.

IBM managers conducted their own VOC research on the best strategies for addressing these market challenges by holding in-depth discussions with an advisory board of IT leaders at midsized companies. The company also conducted extensive market research into buyer trends, priorities, and preferences. The research reinforced that midmarket clients were interested in solutions designed and priced to fit their unique needs; easy access to timely, relevant, helpful information; sales resources that understand their industry; and real-world insight and experience from their peers.

One key result of IBM's VOC research was the decision to partner with CIO.com, the online portal of the highly recognizable magazine for chief information officers, to create infoBOOM! (www.theinfo boom.com): an online gathering place for IT professionals in midsized companies. In IBM's words, infoBOOM! "fosters the free exchange of ideas among experts, midmarket CIOs, and information technology leaders." It also offers powerful firsthand evidence undercutting the preconceptions that many midmarket IT professionals have about IBM.

The program has been rolled out successfully in the United States, the United Kingdom, Belgium, France, Italy, India, Australia and New Zealand, and Singapore. Upcoming deployments include Luxembourg and the Netherlands, China, Germany, Spain, and Spanish-speaking countries in Latin America.

The rollout of the infoBOOM! forum on a global level at an accelerated pace suggests that the results have been positive, with the average time spent within the experience at 11 minutes and a return visitor rate of 65 percent. Additionally, growth in the community has increased consistently each week at a rate of 10 percent.

The forum's purpose is to bring IT professionals the "best of the best"; help them make better decisions; improve the way they do business; and be more successful in the marketplace. It does this by providing the following:

• Advice and opinions from industry experts
• Comments from like-minded peers
• Real insight that can change how the target companies do business

We asked Leslie Reiser, IBM's program director of digital marketing, WW General Business, to share the lessons she has learned from launching the various infoBOOM! social media channels via the official hub, Facebook, and LinkedIn, where it boasts thousands of highly engaged, and highly opinionated, senior IT professionals. She shared the following insights.

COMPANY BRIEFING
SEVEN LESSONS WE LEARNED FROM
LAUNCHING INFOBOOM!
LESLIE REISER, Program Director of Digital Marketing,
WW General Business, IBM

Lesson 1. Start with the customer.

Our initial interviews with CIOs provided us with a great deal of invaluable input that helped direct the launch of the forum. We knew from the beginning that our members' experience had to be rooted in discussions that connected them to the needs and experiences of their fellow participants.

Interviewees told us that they:

- Had limited access to peers and other CIOs—leading to a feeling of being disconnected.

- Wanted access to a deep level of the IBM knowledge base, subject matter experts, and thought leadership to help them with strategy, planning, and other aspects of their job.

- Needed a "safe place" to network with their peers, trusted advisors, IBM experts, and business partners who have faced similar business challenges. They were interested in what those people had learned: what the pitfalls and the best practices were.

- Desired a seat at the strategic decision-making table within their companies. In midmarket, the CIO often wears multiple "hats"—often serving as the IT manager and the network administrator, as well as other roles. As such, the midmarket CIOs look for opportunities that—through the timely delivery of relevant information—can make them more effective and influential in their jobs.

These interviews made it clear that if our community gave users the perspective and knowledge they told us they were seeking, it would be perceived as high value.

Lesson 2. It's important to understand what members of our target market consider to be the "trusted sources" and to build relationships around those sources.

At its heart, social networking is about making connections via recommendations. Aren't you more likely to take an incoming phone call from someone who is personally introduced to you within some social context? The same principle applies to the online world. We are all more inclined to connect with another person via a social network when we're referred to that contact from a trusted source. With infoBOOM! we're always looking for ways to leverage both offline and online social relationships that already exist. This means asking questions such as: How can people use our forum to connect or reconnect with colleagues they already know? Which content experts offer the most relevant experience and insights for our user base? How can we allow users to share their trusted resources with others?

Lesson 3. Issue personalized calls to action.

InfoBOOM! is membership driven and doesn't charge a fee. Our success is measured by our ability to grow the size and quality of our community. Registered members enjoy a wide variety of benefits not always obvious to the casual visitor or user. A strong call to action such as "Ask Kevin Hansen (director of IT for Quadion Corporation) how to optimize Lotus Notes at your company" targets the message while pointing the audience to a new and relevant resource. We have a responsibility to consistently validate that we're delivering on the program's value proposition. This means soliciting feedback via tools like polling, monitoring the number of participants in a live chat, and offering one-on-one feedback to comments posted to a discussion thread. All of these exchanges are indicators that the experience is providing a valuable exchange in return for someone's time.

Lesson 4. Confirm what our customers have already told us. Any blatant attempt to sell or market to the midsized client would result in failure, whereas supporting important discussions would result in success.

Based on the initial feedback from our discussions with IT professionals, we did not want to be perceived as overly IBM-centric; rather, our goal was to encourage commentary about the issues facing IT decision makers in the target market. Our members face tough decisions on complicated issues—this is their opportunity to ask, discuss, and be heard. They tell us what works and what doesn't while we add the features and content they demand. The focus is on providing insights and perspectives on vital issues, not creating purchase points. InfoBOOM! encourages open dialogue and contrary points of view among our editor, experts, and members. Collective participation and feedback are the drivers behind infoBOOM! as it evolves and grows to serve the needs of our community.

Lesson 5. Make it easy for people to leave their mark.

Our goal is to integrate effectively with external social network platforms to generate awareness of our community. This means providing access in multiple social media outlets; it means going where customers are already going for information and discussion. We've taken this approach with infoBOOM! making all aspects of the community experience—access to content, ability to engage with subject matter experts via participation in discussion threads, the ability to ask questions or posting commentary—accessible via Facebook and LinkedIn. People can also follow conversation through the infoBOOM! group on Twitter. We need to think of social networks as not only drive to destination "sites" but as outlets where discussion occurs, based on individual preference. It's immaterial whether a customer engages on our community hub or within Facebook, LinkedIn, or Twitter (where they may already be active). All that matters is that they engage and value the unique perspective given on a topic.

Lesson 6. Let members self-promote.

It's important to remember that we're providing a forum for user-generated content; that's what generates involvement and engagement. Our own research and the feedback we've generated from users have indicated over and over again that community members value having an environment to submit content they created and also receiving the associated self-promotion opportunities for doing so. This capability is a necessary component to building a vibrant and engaging community.

Lesson 7. The people with the loudest voices on site don't necessarily represent the community as a whole.

Social marketing engagement findings indicate that 1 percent of the audience in a given community will contribute, 10 percent will join, and 80 percent will hover, watch, and react. infoBOOM! has been designed to be poised to quickly respond to audience queries. As the participants' behavior begins to shift from merely consuming content to actively contributing content, infoBOOM! encourages engagement within a lively dialogue and promotes the exchange of ideas within the community. At the same time, we have to remain true to the integrity of the value proposition we are offering by leveraging the inherent characteristics of the social web—authenticity and transparency. To this end, it's important not to succumb to sideline influencers with bullhorns when making content choices. There are a lot of armchair quarterbacks in the marketplace who are full of great advice—after the fact. When creating a vibrant community that serves all of our targeted users well, it's best to avoid letting these highly vocal individuals exercise undue influence over what resources are offered and who is offering them. To that end, we keep our original criteria for value delivered—based on our VOC discussions with target users—close at hand, and we continually vet our forum's user experience against those criteria.

IBM's emphasis is on creating and supporting conversations with engaged members of an online community—a vastly different goal than "selling" midlevel IT decision makers on IBM products and services directly. The success of the community at theinfoboom.com reflects an important new responsibility for senior marketing officers. They are now, in addition to their traditional duties, builders of conversations within virtual communities, and aggregators of content of interest to members of those communities.

CASE STUDY:
TINY PRINTS—TARGETING THE CUSTOMER IN THE PRESENT TENSE

CLOSE-UP ON TINY PRINTS
- Founded in 2004
- Headquarters: Mountain View, California
- Online "source for chic and modern stationery for all life occasions"
- Approximately 200 employees
- www.tinyprints.com

In the earlier chapters of this book, we shared the guiding principles behind the critical in-depth research with customers, prospects, and other key players that we call Voice-of-the-Customer Relationship Research. Think of those lengthy one-on-one conversations as "front-end" VOC research.

There's also an obligation and opportunity to listen to customers and other stakeholders in real time as your business moves forward. These exchanges, which don't have to take place voice-to-voice, can often take the form of hard numbers that allow you to analyze all the measurable ways that customers tell you what is important to them. Customers can send you messages in countless ways, and the better you are at understanding those messages, the more value you will derive from the ongoing VOC feedback loop.

Tiny Prints, an online retailer of personalized greeting cards and customized stationery based in Mountain View, California, has won market share by identifying—and acting on—"back-end" VOC guidance. The company has no brick-and-mortar retail facility—and indeed no sales channel besides its Web sites, TinyPrints.com and Wedding PaperDivas.com, which offer two brands of high-end personalized stationery and a revolutionary greeting-card product that's akin to Netflix for greeting cards. The company is a direct competitor with greeting-card giant Hallmark, offering exclusive designs from acclaimed designers, easy card personalization, a powerful preview engine, and world-class customer service. Postings on the Tiny Prints Facebook page give a glimpse of a community of enthusiastic fans who consider each other—and the roughly 200 Tiny Prints employees—something pretty close to family. (Check it out yourself at www.facebook.com/tinyprints, and you'll probably see a fair number of baby pictures.)

Tiny Prints has been profitable since its founding in 2004, in large part because of its use of effective search engine marketing strategies to manage paid search campaigns on Google, Yahoo!, Bing, and a wide range of secondary channels. The company lives or dies on its keyword bids; the information it gathers and analyzes on what its target customers like to click on, and why, constitute one of its central competitive advantages.

We reached out to Anna Fieler, the VP of marketing for Tiny Prints, who brings to Tiny Prints a decade of experience marketing e-commerce companies including eBay and Cafe Press. We asked her to share how she oversees the company's marketing efforts including brand, acquisition, and retention marketing.

C O M P A N Y   B R I E F I N G
HOW TINY PRINTS LISTENS FOR THE
ONLINE VOICE OF THE CUSTOMER
ANNA FIELER, Vice President of Marketing,
Tiny Prints

Tiny Prints' marketing goals are twofold: build brand awareness and a loyal following for our brand, and profitably acquire new customers. One key component of Tiny Prints' growth strategy has been our ability to profitably acquire customers via online performance marketing, especially search marketing. We monitor keyword and visiting patterns carefully, and we also monitor chatter and feedback from customers and prospects in online forums. We pride ourselves in our ability to balance strong customer service that listens to what customers say with some pretty sophisticated analytics that tell us what customers actually want and how they actually behave.

Our search marketing strategy, which is based on identifying the Voice of the Customer online, has three complementary objectives: master search marketing, in both "paid" and "natural" forms; understand customers' search behavior; and execute paid and natural search programs to capture online demand.

Here's a little background on search marketing. "Paid search," also known as "search engine marketing" (SEM) or "pay-per-click" (PPC), is what delivers the "sponsored-links" section on top and to the right when someone does a search for a term on (for instance) Google. This kind of marketing is all about knowing what search terms will be of interest to your prospective customers. "Natural search," also known as "search engine optimization" (SEO), is what yields the "real" Google results on the left, below the sponsored-links section. This kind of marketing is all about influencing where you show up on the search engine results page (or "SERP," as it is referred to by search marketers).

SEM can capture demand almost immediately, but it can be very expensive. SEO can be very efficient in terms of return on investment, but it can be quite difficult to get and keep the high rankings on a page, especially in a competitive space with well-established players. This kind of dominance can take a very long time to build. We believe both need to be part of our mix.

SEM Takeaways

- We analyze the data closely, so we know what words customers use to search for our products online.
- We build and actively manage our keyword portfolio.
- We know the value of each keyword and/or keyword grouping (which keywords convert, at what rate, what average order size, and so forth; also, which keyword groupings are the most valuable beyond the first transaction).
- We set the right cost per acquisition (CPA) goal. How much are you willing to spend to acquire each customer? How does that goal differ based on seasonality, product category, and so forth?
- We set different CPAs based on different goals. There are different philosophies for setting CPA targets depending on your financial goals. You can set a CPA goal based on the goal of being profitable on the first transaction; or you can set a CPA goal to just break even on that first transaction (if you don't care much about making money on the first transaction, and you are willing to bank on the "lifetime value" of the customer, that is, making money when customers return in subsequent transactions). You can even set your CPA goal to break even on your portfolio of keywords, where you might lose money on some keywords and make money on some, but on average, the portfolio breaks even or is profitable for you. This may be an important strategy to use when you need to subsidize certain categories that are expensive to compete in. This concept is akin to the "loss-leader" concept in retail. Your CPA strategy can change, and you can use a mix of different strategies in different parts of your business.

- We monitor our results on a day-by-day, hour-by-hour, and even minute-by-minute basis. It's important to monitor how prospects and customers respond to a keyword in real time, because SEM can be very dynamic given the competitive bidding nature. We've compared SEM to playing a game of chess where the opponent's moves are never quite clear, but you still have to adjust to their effects.

- We test constantly to learn (and fine-tune) what appeals to our customers. For instance: There are many benefits to using Tiny Prints when shopping for holiday cards: premium-quality thick paper stock, selection of thousands of cards in different styles, white-glove customer service, the state-of-the-art personalization platform, and the most stylish designs to be found anywhere on the Internet. We wanted to know: which of these elements appeals the most to customers? Instead of guessing, we created two versions of an online ad copy and created an A/B test. The result: We learned that one message—"Chic, stylish cards, personalize and preview"—outperforms other messaging points by approximately 200 percent.

The SEO Takeaways

- We make sure we know which keywords to optimize for, based on keyword research. For instance, in November and December, the "Christmas cards" search volume is much higher than the volume for "holiday cards." So we work to optimize our site with *new products and content*—in a way that it best helps customers searching for "Christmas cards" meet their intent when they are on our site. In successfully meeting customers' needs with great products and useful content, we have a greater likelihood of winning in SEO.

- We make sure we have a content-rich site that's well organized so that users and Google bots alike can find what they're looking for. Extreme care is taken to ensure that visitors to our site can find the perfect card for them, whether they search by color, collection style, size, or number of photos.

- We get the word out about our brand virally by evangelizing our community of passionate customers and bloggers. This is essential because Google search bots give credit to the number and strength of links to your site.

- We encourage our community of passionate influencers, such as bloggers and loyal customers, to endorse our product and write reviews. Tiny Prints hosts reviews on our site where thousands of customers post reviews of our products; we get an average of 4.8-star ratings out of 5. This is all user-generated content that helps SEO immensely.

- We build the brand by encouraging customers to become a fan of our Tiny Prints Facebook community and follow the Tiny Prints brand on Twitter. "Brand-driven" search marketing campaigns—ones that take advantage of a consumer's willingness to type the words "Tiny Prints" into a search engine rather than "birth announcement"—tend to be more profitable than other online campaigns because they have lower up-front costs and higher conversion rates. It's always in your best interest to build your brand!

Beyond Search: Some Final Thoughts

Search is a great way to capture demand online, but it has its limits. If you need to create demand for your product, search is not the way to do it. So, for instance, if you are launching a brand new product category where there is no search volume because customers don't even know enough about you to search for your product, no amount of SEM or SEO will drive traffic to your site.

In that case, you're probably best off trying to build a great experience that users will want to recommend to others—in other words, you're better off engaging and supporting a community. That's where all the effort's going anyway! Creating that positive experience is still our primary focus at Tiny Prints. We're proud of what we've accomplished in search engine marketing, but we see it as part of an overall process that supports the experience of the people in our community. When someone logs into a mom's forum online and raves about the fact that we sent a blurry picture back to the customer rather than creating a birth announcement around that picture, we take a great deal of pride in that.

NOW WHAT?

- Focus on creating and supporting conversations with engaged members of your audience—a vastly different goal than just "selling" prospects your products and services.
- Consider using VOC research to understand how customers and prospects define a deeper, ongoing relationship with your company and how that should be experienced via social media.
- Find out where your customers and prospects are going to discuss your company and other related firms. Listen, learn, and participate in the dialogue if appropriate.
- Personalize your message and keep it authentic.
- Make it easy for people to leave their mark.
- Create and support an engaged community of fans.
- Learn all you can about the "crowdsourcing" business model. The implications on engaging your community of customers may be profound.
- View the use of SEO and SEM as a numbers-driven science that allows you to target consumers effectively—and capture the Voice of the Customer in real time.

We're not done yet! In the next chapter, you'll learn about the special role VOC-driven social media has to play for nonprofits and social businesses.

CHAPTER

9

LEVERAGING VOC-DRIVEN SOCIAL MEDIA TO CHANGE THE WORLD

EXECUTIVE SUMMARY

- Nonprofits and social businesses face a particularly sensitive set of tasks when it comes to deploying social media.
- Social media engagement with stakeholders must take place on a day-to-day, hour-to-hour, or even minute-to-minute basis. This level of connection is not only recommended for these organizations—it is now mandatory for success.
- Toronto-based Free The Children has built social media into its long-range strategic plan to free children from poverty and exploitation and (just as important) to free young people from the notion that they are powerless to effect positive change in the world.
- California-based TOMS Shoes uses social media to win evangelists for its mission: for every pair of shoes it sells, TOMS gives a pair of shoes to a child in need. The ongoing feedback loop with customers also gives the company some of its best product ideas.

CASE STUDY:
FREE THE CHILDREN

CLOSE-UP ON FREE THE CHILDREN
- Founded in 1995
- Headquarters: Toronto, Ontario, Canada
- Youth-driven children's charity emphasizing sustainable development in marginalized countries
- www.freethechildren.com

Assignment:
Save the World

One day, while reading the Sunday comics in the morning newspaper, 12-year-old Craig Kielburger was stopped cold by a headline that read, "Battled child labor, boy, 12, murdered." Transfixed, he read the story of Iqbal Masih, a Pakistani boy who had escaped child labor at age 10 to become a leader in the movement against bonded labor and child slavery. Masih was shot and killed at age 12 for speaking out.

Craig brought the article into his seventh-grade classroom to ask if anyone would help him continue Iqbal's fight. Eleven hands shot up, and Free The Children was born. Since that day, Craig (now 27) and his friends haven't stopped. He has traveled the world, learning from thousands of forgotten and voiceless people and giving inspirational speeches to world leaders and youth.

Wouldn't it be wonderful if we could capitalize on more visions born "out of the box"? The best source of these visions is available to us in our young people. Their questions do not follow the accepted logic of adults; they venture into new territories with greater imagination.

It's no surprise, then, that youth created many of the most important innovations in contemporary charity. They also invented "social business" and "cause marketing"—long before either term was coined. They did all this from a genuine openness that allowed them to envision great and worthwhile goals: adopting whole villages, building schools and clinics, digging wells, fighting adult illiteracy, and distributing video cameras as tools for constructive change.

There are thousands of examples of the great impact brought by children and teenagers in developing nations. We can find inspiration in their persistence—and in many cases in their power of persuasion. Our young people remain the best proponents of the process of visionary, socially responsible innovation. Free The Children continues to illustrate this magical process, day after day, week after week, and year after year.

—Eva Haller, Social Activist and Chair,
Free The Children USA

Since its founding in 1995, Free The Children has grown into a youth movement that spans the globe. From its headquarters in Toronto, Free The Children has built more than 500 schools in developing countries around the world, providing quality primary education to over 50,000 students every day, and channeling over 90 percent of the cash it collects to the children it has pledged to serve. Sixty to sixty-five percent of the money raised comes directly from youth. Today, Free The Children is the world's largest network of children helping children through education, with more than 1 million youth involved in innovative education and development programs in 45 countries. The group's collection of awards and recognitions is remarkable:

- 2002 World of Children Founders Award
- 2006 World's Children's Prize for the Rights of the Child, also known as the Children's Nobel Prize
- 2006 Human Rights Award from the United Nations and World Association of Non-Government Organizations
- World Economic Forum Medal

- State of the World Forum Award
- Roosevelt Freedom Medal
- Staff members have been honored with Canada's Most Powerful Women: Top 100, Canada's Top 40 under 40, Canada's Top 20 under 20, as well as the Order of Canada.

Our first critical group of stakeholders is kids. Our second is teachers.
                    —CRAIG KIELBURGER, FOUNDER, FREE THE CHILDREN

Free The Children's innovative Global Voices program gives educators free lesson plans that accompany a weekly world issues column that inspires students through issues-based activities and discussion.

Free The Children's primary goals are to free children from poverty and exploitation and (just as important) to free young people from the notion that they are powerless to effect positive change in the world. Through domestic empowerment programs and leadership training, Free The Children inspires young people to develop as socially conscious global citizens and become agents of change for their peers around the world.

The Free The Children team implements its acclaimed Adopt a Village development program in rural and marginalized areas in Kenya, China, India, Sierra Leone, Ecuador, Sri Lanka, and Haiti. Designed to meet the basic needs of developing communities and eliminate the obstacles preventing children from accessing education, Adopt a Village is made up of four pillars crucial to lifting communities from poverty: education, alternative income, health care, and water and sanitation. The Adopt a Village program supports community development in areas where there exists a high incidence of child labor, exploitation of children, and minimal opportunities for the female children. The development program is a true partnership with local communities that are actively consulted and involved throughout the development process.

Engaging the Highly Connected Stakeholder

Here's what founder Craig Kielburger shared with us about Free The Children's social media strategy, which is now a central component of his strategic plan:

"At Free The Children, we are fortunate that our primary audiences are among the most digitally engaged demographics in North America. That makes social media a natural asset for us, as well as an affordable one. We are a nonprofit, so the low initial investments required for our online marketing initiatives hold particular value to us, because they allow us to keep our administrative rate among the lowest in our industry.

"Social media technologies allow us to complement traditional media investments, respond quickly to trends, address changes in audience interest, and assist in rapid response to disasters, such as the devastating earthquake in Haiti or the tsunami in Sri Lanka [see Figure 9.1].

"In addition to sending general e-newsletters and targeted updates to students, educators, and parents, we regularly provide promotional 'blasts' whenever big events occur or pertinent news arises. One notable aspect of our e-mail strategy is the speed with which we can contact those who have attended a Free The Children event or speaking engagement. Within one week of any event, individuals who expressed interest in learning more receive both an e-mail and a phone call to help them build an action plan. This serves as the first step to engagement and involvement with Free The Children.

"This strategy of quick engagement has taken on an exciting new dimension with our efforts in social media because of the staggering number of youth who now use tools like Facebook on a daily basis. Over the last year, we have centralized what were previously a disparate group of separate Web forums and a wide range of Facebook groups into a strong, consolidated, and carefully coordinated online presence.

"Through Facebook and Twitter, we can now post micro-updates to our constituents about anything and everything—from goings on around the office to new campaign videos, from updates from our projects around the world to details about something I've personally seen

Figure 9.1: An e-mail message from Free The Children. Notice how easy it is for recipients to click on a logo and follow the organization's activities on Facebook, YouTube, and Twitter.

unfolding while I'm out traveling. We also use social media as a management tool. Our young team of youth programming coordinators pays close attention to the various social networks, answering the many questions that people ask in these online spaces.

"Another strong push that we have made over the past year is in our use of online video. Video allows us to tell the story of Free The Children to new audiences in succinct, engaging ways. Video is proving to be a particularly effective resource when it comes to helping our active members with their fund-raising and awareness activities. Young people show our YouTube videos to friends, we're able to provide links to the videos on our Facebook pages, and we can use e-mail and other contact methods to get teachers to show appropriate videos to their classes. YouTube noticed our success on their site, and it profiled us for the launch of their Canadian nonprofit program. What's more, our ability to use the Internet to transfer videos from the field quickly enables us to provide timely and engaging updates to our donors, showing them in a powerful and engaging way, exactly what the impact their donations and actions look like. This is a great way to keep them involved.

"Of particular benefit to nonprofits are the powerful analytic tools that come with virtually zero cost on all these online channels. Facebook, for instance, provides us with immediate feedback, through comments and the 'like' feature, and it also delivers powerful demographic data about who is paying attention to us online and how much they are responding to each post. Similarly, YouTube not only lets us see similar demographic information but it also provides the added benefit of showing us how people are finding our videos and how much attention they are paying at different points throughout a given video.

During the academic year of 2009 to 2010, the Free The Children YouTube channel inspired over 240,000 views. (That total will be higher by the time you read this; see for yourself by visiting www.youtube.com/freethechildrenintl).

"Obviously, what we hear from stakeholders through these new media channels is just as important as the messages we send. Twitter is a particularly great listening tool for nonprofits. During our signature event, We Day, our Web site is filled with tweets from the thousands of attendees who post their immediate reactions as they take in the speakers and performers during the event. This gives us indispensable real-time feedback about what we're doing—what's working and what isn't.

"Data from social media tools allowed us to revise the freethechildren.com Web site in a way that takes into account our different core audiences, focuses on their most asked questions, delivers their most requested resources, and allows us to analyze how users actually navigate the site. Following the lead of kids who used these tools, we massively ramped up the 'sharability' of our content, increasing the presence of our social media channels and embedding easily sharable YouTube videos on dozens of pages throughout the site.

"Facebook is increasingly important for us because Facebook takes time for people to set up and is thus less likely to be abandoned and replaced by some other platform. What's more, young people today conduct a whole lot of social interaction through that one platform. Our experience is that young people are much more likely to use Facebook on a daily basis than Twitter. Facebook gives you a clearer sense of whom you're dealing with than Twitter—or e-mail, for that matter. Young people are likely to launch and abandon e-mail addresses with great frequency (which makes them hard for us to follow using that information), and they also tend to use names that bear no relation to their actual identity (a problem that plays out on Twitter, as well). Facebook gives you a much lower turnover rate, it shows you more clearly whom you're dealing with, and it gives you a more stable environment in which to communicate.

"Another big advantage of Facebook is that it allows you to create pages for the key people operating within your organization, people who can create powerful individual relationships with your stakeholders. The big distinction here is that people tend to bond most strongly with other people, and less strongly with organizations. Now, it's not that we don't want people to keep up with our Free The Children page on Facebook—it's wonderful if they choose to do that. But we also want to give kids the option to connect one-on-one once they've heard someone like Michel Chikwanine speak on a very personal level about what it was like to survive civil war, political upheaval, and poverty in the Democratic Republic of the Congo. We want kids to be able to use Facebook to establish a personal connection with speakers like him; that's going to be an important relationship because Michel is only slightly older than a lot of the kids we talk to. So once someone makes that one-on-one connection with Michel, he or she is much more likely to be interested in what he's up to, what he's seeing, what he's doing, than in hearing from some organizational persona.

"The same principle applies to the people who are leading our efforts in the field. For instance, Robin Wiszowaty is our Kenya program director. Ideally, we'd like as many of our stakeholders as possible to be a friend with her on a personal level on Facebook. What's going to have more impact? Us releasing a press release about how there's a shortage of basic medical supplies in Kenya? Or her leaving a post to all of her friends on Facebook, explaining that it really breaks her heart not to be able to help the sick kids she's seeing? Ultimately, people resonate with people. They don't resonate with brands so much.

> *Ultimately, people resonate with people. They don't resonate with brands so much.*
> —CRAIG KIELBURGER

"Moving forward, Free The Children seeks to tighten the interaction of all our online properties. Our goal is to cultivate an active user base of young leaders and change makers who are ready to take action, and social media will continue to be a part of that goal. Free The Children will pursue its mission by continuing to expand its activities— both globally and in the online space. As I see it, those two expansions must take place simultaneously.

"Social media now play a leading role in driving Free The Children's annual 'We Day,' one of the major annual media events in Canada and a major landmark on the North American charitable calendar. Free The Children's We Day is more than just one day of celebration and inspiration. It's a one-of-a-kind event and part of an innovative yearlong program created to celebrate the power of young people to create positive change in the world. We Day is free of charge and open to any school that wants to be part of the experience. In exchange, each school group that attends is asked to make a commitment to follow the We Schools in Action program, which includes taking local and global action throughout the year."

BY THE NUMBERS: FREE THE CHILDREN ORGANIZATION SINCE 2007

- Over 23,000 people have become fans of the Free The Children Facebook page.
- 51,400 students from across Canada have attended We Day events, and they brought back the message to their schools, impacting hundreds of thousands more.
- Participating students collectively fund-raised to support Free The Children's Adopt a Village development program.
- More than $5 million has been raised by participating students for diverse charities.
- Young people volunteered more than 150,000 hours to benefit over 500 charities and community groups. Fueled by social media connections, that growth has been exponential; it's estimated that Free The Children volunteers will log a total of 1 million volunteer hours by the end of the 2009 and 2010 school year.

Craig Kielburger's Key Takeaways

- Ensure that you use social media to both reach out to your community members and learn from them in terms of what they consider relevant. This is about a two-way conversation.
- Use social media sites such as Twitter and Facebook to engage stakeholders, particularly younger stakeholders.
- Social media allow for targeted lists of engaged people. Respect the trust and communicate only what is relevant.
- Speed to market is a critical factor; it helps reinforce your relevance.

- Ramp up the "sharability" of your content.
- Use social media's low-cost measurement tools to synchronize your message and streamline communications to your stake-holders.
- Give people both a good cause and a cool experience they can talk about (and text about, and Facebook about) with their friends for months or years to come. The event you sponsor may last a day . . . but the ongoing discussions about the emotions of that day should go on for much longer than that.
- Use social media to stay connected and stay transparent. Perceived (or actual) disengagement from the stakeholder means asking for trouble in the social media era—the kind of trouble that most nonprofits and social businesses can't afford.

CASE STUDY:
TOMS SAYS, SHOES MATTER

CLOSE-UP ON TOMS SHOES
- Founded in 2006
- Headquarters: Santa Monica, California
- Nonprofit subsidiary: Friends of TOMS
- Facebook fans: Over 300,000
- Operating model: With every pair of shoes sold, TOMS donates a new pair of shoes to a child in need.
- Web site: www.toms.com
- Outlets: In addition to the official TOMS Shoes Web site, TOMS are sold in retail stores in over 20 countries worldwide, including the United Kingdom, Japan, Sweden, Germany, Italy, South Korea, and Australia.

TOMS Shoes is a footwear manufacturer and social activist. The company combines marketing savvy with a profound, and impossible-to-forget, charitable impulse: for every pair of shoes it sells, TOMS gives a pair of shoes to a child in need.

WHY SHOES?

Using the purchasing power of individuals to benefit the greater good is what we're all about. The TOMS One for One movement transforms our customers into benefactors, which allows us to grow a truly sustainable business rather than depending on fundraising for support.

Why shoes? Because many children in developing countries grow up barefoot. Whether at play, doing chores, or going to school, these children are at risk. A leading cause of disease in developing countries is soil-transmitted diseases, which can penetrate the skin through bare feet. Wearing shoes can help prevent these diseases, and the long-term physical and cognitive harm they cause. Wearing shoes also prevents feet from getting cuts and sores. Not only are these injuries painful; they also are dangerous when wounds become infected. Often children can't attend school barefoot because shoes are a required part of their uniform. If they don't have shoes, they don't go to school. If they don't receive an education, they don't have the opportunity to realize their potential.

—From the TOMS Shoes Web site

TOMS founder Blake Mycoskie got the big idea while on vacation in Argentina in January 2006. As he later recalled: "I was sitting on a farm pondering life, and it occurred to me, 'I'm going to start a shoe company, and for every pair that we sell, I'll give a pair to someone who needs them.'" Mycoskie based the company's shoe designs on the popular alpargata shoes he saw while in Argentina.

"What we do at TOMS," he told us in a recent interview, "is find ways to allow our customers to participate in giving shoes to the people who need them. That's how we stay close to our constituency, and that's how we get our message across. We also take many of our customers with us on trips all around the world to give away shoes to kids who need them. These customers then share videos, photos, and blog postings at TOMSshoes.com, or via Facebook, Twitter, or other platforms. We use social media to involve the customer every step of the way—no pun intended.

"It's probably a 50-50 split between people who initially buy shoes from us for the fashion and people who initially buy shoes from us for the cause. What we find is that these two constituencies are constantly merging. There are many people who initially buy for the cause, and they end up falling in love with the fashion and the comfort of the shoes; by the same token, there are a lot of people who get to know TOMS because they love the way the shoes look and feel, and they end up wanting to learn more about the cause. There's a lot of cross-pollination involved."

BY THE NUMBERS: TOMS SHOES

- Approximately 300,000 participants in One Day Without Shoes, 2010; up from 50,000 in 2009
- 800+ high school and college clubs focused on the TOMS Shoes mission
- 30,000+ guests on the One Day Without Shoes Facebook page
- 600,000 shoes given away to children in need

Barefoot for the Cause

We asked Mycoskie to give us an example of social media's role in galvanizing and focusing the TOMS community, and it didn't take him long to come up with one. "We have a big event, one day a year, called One Day Without Shoes, where we encourage the whole world to go barefoot. It's coordinated through a special Web site, OneDay WithoutShoes.com, which gives people the chance to register and organize a barefoot walk. So by going to school, or to work, or to some other destination barefoot, you obviously get people asking the question: Why? And that's the opportunity to share the message about what it's like for children to live a life without shoes full time. That's one big way we call attention to the TOMS movement. We had about 300,000 people to participate this year; last year we had 50,000 people taking part. That kind of exponential growth in a single year was only possible because of communication tools like Facebook and Twitter."

The One Day Without Shoes Facebook page boasts over 30,000 guests as of this book's press time, as well as tons of photos posted by people who have taken part in One Day Without Shoes or are contemplating doing so in the future. The annual event not only raises awareness for the TOMS mission but also raises sales and visibility.

TOMS BEGS CONSUMERS: STOP USING OUR PRODUCT!

One Day Without Shoes is the day we spread awareness about the impact a simple pair of shoes can have on a child's life. On April 8, we ask people to go the day, part of the day, or even just a few minutes, barefoot, to experience firsthand a life without shoes and to inspire others at the same time. Pledge your support! RSVP and be entered to win a spot on a TOMS Shoe Drop, all expenses paid. (A Shoe Drop is a trip to distribute shoes to children.) Through everyday encounters with domestic poverty, we are reminded to appreciate having food and shelter, but most of us all but forget about our feet. Food, shelter, AND shoes facilitate life's fundamentals. Imagine a life without shoes; constantly aware of the ground in front of you, suffering regular cuts and scrapes, tending to infection after each walk, and enduring not only terrain but heat and cold.

The problem is large, but the solution is simple. Wearing shoes and practicing basic hygiene can prevent both infection and disease due to unsafe roads and contaminated soil. By imagining a life barefoot, we can all contribute to the awareness of these conditions. On April 8, communities, campuses, organizations, and individuals are banding together to walk barefoot for One Day Without Shoes. Take a walk with us on April 8!

—From OneDayWithoutShoes.com

The upshot is that once a year, TOMS Shoes gets thousands of people to take off their shoes, walk out of the house, and overcome the nagging fear that others will look at them funny for striding around with no shoes on all day long—which they will. Why do people do this? Because they've been engaged at a personal level, typically by friends who want to share the experience of supporting the cause for which the company was founded. And because they like sharing the experience with others. Each and every one of these barefoot evangelists is making a public statement about helping kids . . . and, in so doing, helping to build the TOMS brand. It's a potent combination.

Here's a blog posting from Lacie, one of the TOMS faithful, about the great day. Notice the communal nature of her adventure—and her eagerness to share it with the world!

As it got closer and closer to One Day Without Shoes, I got more and more excited. My roommate and I made shirts to wear that day and help people understand that we had a purpose and weren't just walking around barefoot for no reason.

The day started off fine, no problems not wearing shoes. Then it was time to walk to class. It was amazing how quickly you figure out what types of pavement are comfortable to walk on and which are not. I got some strange looks from my teachers, but I took it as another opportunity to spread our message. A few of my classmates, upon hearing the cause and what I was doing, immediately took their shoes off and started spreading the word too.

On the way from class to class, strangers would stop and ask questions like, "Do you not own any shoes?" I answered, "I do, but I'm walking for the kids that don't." . . . I got nearly 20 new people to walk barefoot by the end of the day!

After walking, we all circled up and talked about our day, shared our experiences, and laughed at the silly questions and strange looks we received on our One Day Without Shoes. That day lit the fire in me to really step it up and make a difference. We can all go one day without shoes, and I think everyone should just so they can realize how TOMS helps those children who don't have shoes.

Market Insights from Social Media

Another example of the power of tapping in to the Voice of the Customer is reflected in the following true story. Facebook, e-mails, and other communications started carrying a common theme: lots of women, as much as they loved TOMS, weren't wearing TOMS because they didn't wear flats.

TOM's designed a wedge, the Argentina espadrille wedge heel. They took them to the largest retail buyers, who were very interested. TOMS said they would manufacture them if the buyers placed large enough advance orders—which was probably a safe bet based on the social media feedback. To date, TOMS has sold more of these shoes in preorders than any shoe to date!

BLAKE MYCOSKIE'S
SEVEN KEY TENETS OF TOMS' SUCCESS

1. *Treat customers like friends and evangelists.* People don't want to just buy stuff anymore; we all want to be part of movements. A customer is a nameless and faceless person with a credit card who buys from you because your stuff is the cheapest and/or most convenient. The minute your prices increase or you become a tad less convenient, customers will gladly take their business elsewhere. Friends and evangelists, by contrast, are loyal to you if you are transparent and loyal to them. They blog and tweet and recommend your product to friends because they love what your company represents.

2. *Create shared goals with retailers.* They want to be friends and evangelists too! When a store carries TOMS, it doesn't do so because our shoes will make the store the most amount of money. Our goal is always to work with retailers and allow them to share in the joy of giving shoes to children in need. There is a direct correlation between how excited a retailer is about TOMS and how many shoes they sell.

3. *Encourage customers to go on Shoe Drops.* Shoe Drops are such memorable and personal trips that it only seems natural that participants (that is, customers) blog, tweet, and post pictures

about their experience putting shoes on children's feet. This is not just free advertisement for TOMS; it's the most powerful form of advertising imaginable at any price. In an era of information overload, we rely more than ever on the advice of our friends and family.

4. *Create a conversation with customers.* It used to be that big brands talked at customers, saturating us with TV and radio ads promoting average products for average people. Because of the fragmentation of media, this type of communication isn't possible anymore, and even if it were, it wouldn't work. Tools like YouTube, Twitter, and Facebook allow you to reach a seemingly unlimited audience for free, but they're only effective if you create a dialogue with your supporters.

5. *Keep things simple and transparent.* The beauty of the TOMS' business model is that everyone can understand it. Were we just a shoe company that gave a percentage of sales to a charity, few people would be emotionally drawn to our cause and want to evangelize on our behalf.

6. *Be remarkable and people will want to talk about you.* Whereas some companies pay thousands of dollars to advertise in the media, TOMS has been featured in some of the top magazines, TV shows, and newspapers for free by virtue of the fact that our story is so compelling. Getting press has nothing to do with how big you are, or how large your advertising budget is. It's all about how emotionally you connect with supporters (and thereby the media).

7. *Incorporate giving into everything that you do.* When TOMS first started, many traditional "businesspeople" thought that One for One was a nice idea that would never work from a financial perspective. What we've found is exactly the opposite. What makes TOMS so special is our commitment to the One for One giving. The moral: Making money and making the world a better place don't have to be mutually exclusive. The success of TOMS shows that you can do both at the same time!

> ### NOW WHAT?
>
> - Use social media to stay connected. Perceived (or actual) disengagement from the stakeholder means asking for trouble in the social media era—the kind of trouble that most nonprofits and social businesses can't afford.
> - Use social media to demonstrate transparency, accountability, and mission commitment to your critical stakeholders—and everyone else.
> - Be remarkable and people will want to talk about you. Getting press has nothing to do with how big you are, or how large your advertising budget is. It's all about how emotionally you connect with supporters (and the media).
> - Ensure that you use social media to both reach out to your community members and learn from them in terms of what they consider relevant. This is about a two-way conversation.
> - Social media allow for targeted lists of engaged people. Respect the trust and communicate only what is relevant.
> - Encourage people to follow individual personalities who are strongly associated with your organization's mission.
> - Celebrate good ideas you receive from customers and stakeholders via social media.

In the next section of the book, you'll learn about the final step in the VOC process: customer service. Yes, it is emphatically a marketing responsibility!

INVEST IN AN EXCELLENT CUSTOMER SERVICE EXPERIENCE

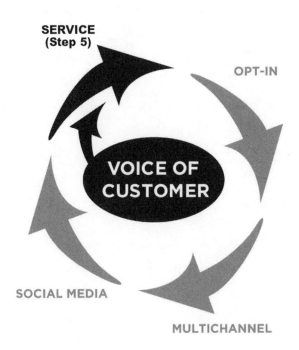

10

CUSTOMER SERVICE: A MARKETING RESPONSIBILITY

EXECUTIVE SUMMARY

- Customers expect high-quality postsale support. If it is lacking, they will not only be inclined to go elsewhere but they will also be inclined to use the power of social media to let a lot of people know about their dissatisfaction.
- We urge you to view customer service as a critical part of the marketing process.
- VOC-driven customer service is a strategic marketing differentiator that can move people through the customer life cycle so effectively that it ensures repeat business and higher rates of renewals, and it provides the additional power of customers' word-of-mouth recommendations.
- By recognizing the importance of customer service years ago and making it an integral part of its customer retention strategies, QVC has built VOC-driven service into its business model—and established a powerful competitive advantage.

Marketers invest untold amounts of time, effort, and energy into the job of *winning* customers. Then, all too often, those same marketers effectively abandon the task of *retaining* those customers by convincing themselves that "customer service is an operations responsibility."

Customer service is, in fact, a marketing responsibility. Often, key people in organizations forget this, especially marketers, and the result is a form of self-inflicted damage as old as marketing itself: unacceptably high rates of customer churn.

According to Dow Jones Interactive, *companies lose 50 percent of their customers every five years!* One major factor: relationships do not extend past the initial sale. Given the amount of work we do to win a customer, this is certainly alarming—but is this all that surprising? Consider the benchmarks for customer retention in the box "Customer Retention by the Numbers," and ask yourself how many of them your organization is currently hitting.

CUSTOMER RETENTION BY THE NUMBERS

How well does your organization match up?
- Optimum average speed of answer on a call to customer service (for minimum 80 percent of calls): 30 to 40 seconds
- Optimum average call abandon rate: 2 percent or less
- Maximum annual turnover rate for customer service representatives (CSRs): 10 to 20 percent
- Optimum response time for an e-mail inquiry: 4 hours

THE EXPERIENCE GAP

Customers are every company's most valuable asset. Now more than ever, companies need to retain existing customers and to attract new ones in order to survive and grow.

Companies know that. And many companies and their management acknowledge this fact in their communications, in corporate brochures, in speeches, and at company and public events.

But what kind of experiences are they actually providing their customers? How are customers actually being treated?

According to Bernd Schmitt, author of the books *Experiential Marketing* and *Customer Experience Management*, "Customers are often treated badly. Think of waiting in lines in supermarkets or on the phone. Think of electronics products that are complicated to use. Think of Web sites where it is hard to find useful information, or uninspiring ad campaigns, or unresponsive—or nonexistent—customer service."

Some companies deliver a great experience that gives them a sustainable competitive advantage (see Figure 10.1). For example, Singapore Airlines is known for its superb in-flight service. Amazon.com has an amazing tracking system and provides a sophisticated system of automated recommendations to customers on what they may want to buy next. Google offers a great, and supremely user friendly, search engine.

Why can't more companies take the customer experience seriously? In Schmitt's view, a lack of understanding of the customer experience is not just an incidental failure. It's not just that a Web site is poorly managed, or that the agent at the call center had a bad day, or that a particular product had a glitch. In many cases, these failures are symptomatic of a broader problem in the organization: the lack of a culture that focuses on and serves customers, internal or external.

So what does it take to change that culture? How can a customer experience be managed and improved?

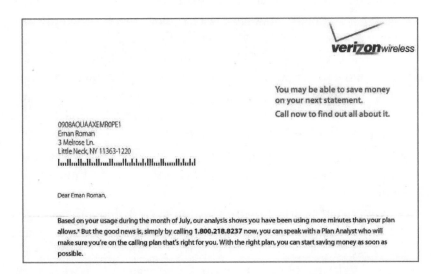

Figure 10.1: When was the last time your customers received a customer service message like this—one that was clearly relevant to his or her world, actions, and choices?

What many companies need is a management framework and implementation tools that focus on the customer experience at every touch point. Schmitt developed such a customer-focused approach, called customer experience management, or simply CEM.

According to Schmitt, the CEM process is composed of five steps.

Step 1, "Analyzing the Experiential World of the Customer," provides original insight into the customer's world. It consists of a systematic audit that assesses how customers are being treated at all touch points and how they should be treated to be delighted.

Step 2, "Building the Experiential Platform," provides a multidimensional depiction of the desired experience and a specification of the experiential value that the customer can expect from the product or service.

For example, Puma, the German athletic shoemaker's experiential platform is not just about "quality" or "innovation." Puma wants to be a "brand that mixes the influences of sports, lifestyle, and fashion." To deliver this value promise, Puma collaborates with international fashion designers. The colors of the shoes have cool names like "gray/camel," "wine/purple," "yellow/apricot," and "violet/tan." The shoes are distributed in high-end boutiques and department stores.

Step 3, "Designing the Brand Experience," includes the quality and design of a product that delivers the experience (Puma's shoe designs and colors). The brand experience also includes the "look and feel" of packaging and retail spaces, and online and offline communications.

Step 4, "Structuring the Customer Interface," includes the dynamic exchanges and contact points with the customer, whether they happen face-to-face in a store, during a sales visit in a client's office, at an automatic teller machine at a bank, at a call center, or as part of Web sites or new media.

Finally, in Step 5, the experiential platform must be reflected in a company's innovation strategy—a process called "Engaging in Continuous Innovation."

Becoming truly customer focused is not easy. As long as a company is internally focused in its product development, marketing and sales, and customer service, it will miss key customer input and the chance of differentiating itself from competition in a relevant way.

THE MARKETING CONTINUUM

VOC-driven customer service is a strategic marketing differentiator that can move people through the customer life cycle so effectively that it ensures repeat business and the additional power of their word-of-mouth recommendations. Effective marketing and customer service can engage customers to move through these phases:

Suspect → prospect → initial user → customer → evangelist/advocate

Figure 10.2 is a detailed visual summary of this process, created by Harvey Markovitz, clinical assistant professor of marketing and the director of the Interactive & Direct Marketing (IDM) Lab, Lubin School of Business, Pace University.

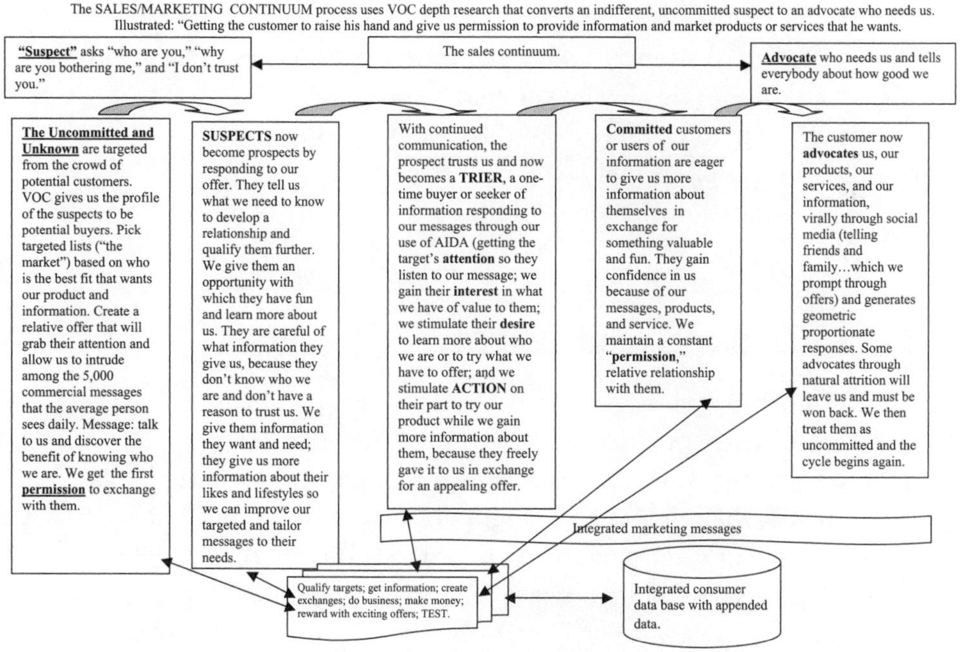

The SALES/MARKETING CONTINUUM process uses VOC depth research that converts an indifferent, uncommitted suspect to an advocate who needs us. Illustrated: "Getting the customer to raise his hand and give us permission to provide information and market products or services that he wants.

The sales continuum.

"Suspect" asks "who are you," "why are you bothering me," and "I don't trust you."

Advocate who needs us and tells everybody about how good we are.

The Uncommitted and Unknown are targeted from the crowd of potential customers. VOC gives us the profile of the suspects to be potential buyers. Pick targeted lists ("the market") based on who is the best fit that wants our product and information. Create a relative offer that will grab their attention and allow us to intrude among the 5,000 commercial messages that the average person sees daily. Message: talk to us and discover the benefit of knowing who we are. We get the first **permission** to exchange with them.

SUSPECTS now become prospects by responding to our offer. They tell us what we need to know to develop a relationship and qualify them further. We give them an opportunity with which they have fun and learn more about us. They are careful of what information they give us, because they don't know who we are and don't have a reason to trust us. We give them information they want and need; they give us more information about their likes and lifestyles so we can improve our targeted and tailor messages to their needs.

With continued communication, the prospect trusts us and now becomes a **TRIER**, a one-time buyer or seeker of information responding to our messages through our use of AIDA (getting the target's **attention** so they listen to our message; we gain their **interest** in what we have of value to them; we stimulate their **desire** to learn more about who we are or to try what we have to offer; and we stimulate **ACTION** on their part to try our product while we gain more information about them, because they freely gave it to us in exchange for an appealing offer.

Committed customers or users of our information are eager to give us more information about themselves in exchange for something valuable and fun. They gain confidence in us because of our messages, products, and service. We maintain a constant **"permission,"** relative relationship with them.

The customer now **advocates** us, our products, our services, and our information, virally through social media (telling friends and family…which we prompt through offers) and generates geometric proportionate responses. Some advocates through natural attrition will leave us and must be won back. We then treat them as uncommitted and the cycle begins again.

Integrated marketing messages

Qualify targets; get information; create exchanges; do business; make money; reward with exciting offers; TEST.

Integrated consumer data base with appended data.

Figure 10.2: The Marketing Communication Management Process

Source: Copyright HBM Associates, Inc., New York, 2002.

Here's What Often Happens Instead

ERDM has conducted industry-recognized research illustrating the alarming state of most customer experiences. Here's what we've found: Most customers receive generic, untargeted messaging that does not clearly reflect their past choices, activities, or preferences. As a result, too many of their experiences are typically unmemorable, or memorable for all the wrong reasons.

In addition:

- Our Call Center Research shows that 66 percent of customers rated their past customer service call center experience as negative or neutral.
- Bad customer service call center experiences negatively affect customers':
  o Willingness to buy from that company: 86 percent
  o Perception of that company: 99 percent
  o Likelihood to recommend the company: 92 percent
- Excellent customer service call center experiences, on the other hand, positively affect customers':
  o Willingness to buy from that company: 80 percent
  o Perception of that company: 94 percent
  o Likelihood to recommend the company: 81 percent

WHAT CUSTOMERS EXPECT

Customers are clear about what makes for a good customer service call center experience. According to our research:
- 63 percent want an easy menu with minimum "clutter" that enables them to reach the right customer service rep
- 65 percent want a rep who understands their needs
- 62 percent want a rep who speaks clearly and is easy to understand
- 67 percent want their issue handled in a single call

Source: Ernan Roman Direct Marketing

A MODEST PROPOSAL:
THE CUSTOMER SERVICE BILL OF RIGHTS

I created this provocative list of customer rights back in 2006; it's been circulating on the Internet since then—and, perhaps, changing perspectives. Don't these seven rights describe how *you* would like to be treated as a customer?

1. To have my precious time respected by the company's customer service department in every situation and to have my issue resolved in a single phone call or e-mail, preferably by one representative who speaks clearly, is easy to understand, and has access to my customer records.

2. To be treated with courtesy and respect as a customer who paid money to the company with the expectation of customer service that cares about my individual needs.

3. To have adequately trained representatives who are empowered enough to actually solve my problem and who will provide me with a case number I can use for a credit if I do not receive great service, as well as the ability to call back or e-mail the same representative should the need arise.

4. To receive quality customer service—including an easy-to-use menu with a minimum of clutter to quickly reach a representative—OR be compensated for my time and effort.

5. To have rapid access to a live person from a company with sufficient staff so I am not kept waiting on hold for more than five minutes, or I will receive a negotiable credit on my next bill. I also have the right to receive a negotiable credit on my next bill from the company if the first customer service rep does not have my records or cannot solve my problem and has to transfer me.

6. To receive a negotiable credit on my next bill from the company if I have to speak with more than two customer service representatives trying to resolve my issue. I also have the right to receive a negotiable credit on my next bill from the company if I ask for a supervisor and none is available.

7. To receive a negotiable credit on my next bill from the company if I am billed incorrectly and I have to call or e-mail to fix the

problem, or I am given the wrong information to fix my problem by any of their representatives, compelling me to call back or send another e-mail.

All of us are consumers, and all of us understand what we expect when we buy something. It comes as no surprise, however, that most marketing organizations fail to meet the core expectations of their customers when it comes to the service experience.

SEVEN WAYS TO OUT-SERVICE THE COMPETITION

1. Accelerate customer loyalty and company profits.
2. Enhance the customer experience and save money.
3. Close the gaps between expectation and experience.
4. Leverage empathetic and emotional experiences.
5. Improve the multichannel experience.
6. Leverage a centralized knowledge base.
7. Use customer insight to drive agility.

Source: Peppers & Rogers Group

CASE STUDY:
QVC

CLOSE-UP ON QVC
- Founded in 1986
- Headquarters: West Chester, Pennsylvania
- Global leader in televised home shopping
- As of this writing, an estimated 60 million people have shopped with QVC.

The following is a world-class example of a company that out-services many consumer marketers: QVC, the TV and online shopping network whose initials stand for Quality, Value, and Convenience. We asked John Hunter, executive vice president of customer fulfillment services, to share some of his company's insights and best practices. Hunter oversees QVC's customer service, distribution, business analysis and engineering, and quality assurance teams, which includes the company's three call centers and four distribution centers.

COMPANY BRIEFING
QVC—PUTTING THE CUSTOMER FIRST
JOHN HUNTER, Executive Vice President of Customer Fulfillment Services, QVC

QVC is one of the largest multimedia retailers in the world, providing its customers with thousands of innovative and contemporary beauty, fashion, jewelry, and home products. Its programming is distributed to more than 180 million homes worldwide, and its Web site, QVC.com, is ranked among the top general merchant Internet sites. QVC has subsidiaries in the United Kingdom, Germany, and Japan, and it is launching in Italy in late 2010. QVC operations in West Chester, Pennsylvania, have shipped more than a billion packages.

The Marketing Challenge

In the early days of QVC, we considered ourselves a customer-driven organization, but we lacked structure. We had devised no real strategy to keep our customers as satisfied and loyal as possible. In spirit, we were customer driven, but in terms of execution, we were like many other companies—we had no operational model to follow, and to build on.

We wanted to be customer driven in more than spirit. The Voice of the Customer had to be imbued within every employee.

And then in 1991, our metrics told us that QVC was growing but not as quickly as we knew it could. This was five years after the company's founding by Joseph Segel, a pioneer who had married technology with a favorite American pastime, shopping.

Concerned? No. Challenged? Absolutely.

The metrics we saw represented an opportunity devised in marketing heaven. It was a chance to claim the money we were leaving on the table, to grow our loyal customer base.

A Different View

At one time, marketers talked about customer satisfaction, and many still do. But most have never connected that satisfaction to behavior—repeat purchasing, and then picking up the phone to tell a friend about the great deal they just got, and how well they were treated by the company.

Part of customer satisfaction is the quality of the product and the service customers receive.

In fact, many companies still view customer service as a necessary evil for handling customer transitions after a sale has been made. Their customer service call centers and Web sites are reduced to a series of tasks and metrics that are focused on talk time, cost of calls, and an endless series of interactive voice response unit prompts.

This narrow view of both service generally and the customer specifically prevents companies from using the customer experience to generate real customer loyalty and to change customer behavior.

It is striking to consider the sheer volume of marketing dollars and effort companies spend to acquire new customers or for enticements used to generate repeat business, while at the same time investing woefully little in their customer service call centers and Web sites to improve the customer experience. The result: the company ends up lending a deaf ear to its customers' needs and failing to retain the sale and its customers.

Leaving customer satisfaction to operations just doesn't make sense.

We were never one of those companies that saw customer service as a necessary evil; now, however, we were looking at it as a way to increase our bottom line. And to do that, the responsibility of providing excellent customer service would belong to all departments, not only ours.

But first, we had to know what the customers wanted. So we set up focus groups in five major U.S. cities. We wanted to know where people shopped, how they shopped, and what they wanted from those they were buying from.

From what we heard in those focus groups, we devised dozens of questions to ask 1,500 customers. We wanted to capture the whole customer experience, from the initial phone call to the purchase, to the product's arrival, so those questions involved every department that touched the customers.

This was our first VOC research survey.

VOC Research

It was obvious from the start that customers were happy to participate; we had a 70 percent take rate. We read that as: We really like you, but we really want to love you.

It was humbling to learn how customers defined a problem and how different it was from our internal business metrics. Before, we had measured things like talk time, while the customers measured our ability to solve problems. We assessed things like percent of packages processed in our distribution centers within 48 hours—but the customers measured delivery accuracy and timeliness. We looked at abandon rates and average speed of answer, while customers were more concerned about their ability to reach a representative in a timely manner and getting their problem solved in one call with minimal effort.

Our research demonstrated that we had a serious disconnect between what we thought was important and what our customers wanted. We had been measuring numbers, and our customers were judging us on the quality of the experience.

We would never become customer driven this way.

The danger of measuring traditional metrics, such as talk time and calls processed per hour, is that they can do a great disservice to the customers if they take priority over the quality of the call or improving the customer interaction. Talk time alone can be a disastrous metric because it can make the customer representative sound robotic. More often than not, it simply doesn't provide for a good customer experience.

Quantifying the Value of Good Customer Service

We were learning what behaviors would lead our customers to recommending us to others, and what would keep them coming back for more purchases. Our senior management was impressed, but not enough to be convinced to invest more in customer service. "Prove it to us," they said. "Prove that if you do X, Y, and Z, that those customers will keep coming back."

So, a year after the initial survey, we contacted those 1,500 customers *again*. And here's what we found: Those people who had said we were excellent, who had rated us at a 7—meaning excellent on a scale of 1 to 7, with 7 being excellent—actually reordered at a rate of 93 percent. This contrasted sharply with customers who rated us a 6, or very good, who reordered at a rate of 78 percent, almost a 15 percent difference.

Customers who rated us a 5, or adequate, only repurchased at a rate of 57 percent.

Clearly we aren't big fans of merging the top two box scores in customer research surveys—because of the significant differences that show up between a 6 and a 7!

What we also found: losing a customer is more costly than gaining a new customer—two and a half times higher. (In other industries, that rate can go as high as seven times.)

Losing a customer is between two and a half and seven times more costly than gaining a new customer.

The message was clear: allocate more resources to keep our customers satisfied. Clearly, new customer acquisition is a key part of a company's growth strategy; we would never argue against that. We would just argue in favor of a better balance of resources.

What Our Customers Want

We think it's important to see how other companies conduct customer research and to understand the impact of service issues on customer loyalty. In many organizations the customer satisfaction list will be different; for us, it's been important to focus on those core customer expectations that, when we've consistently delivered at a high level, have become service differentiators. Every company should go through this exercise.

This is what QVC customers want:

- Customers expect minimal or no service issues to be experienced. If they do experience an issue, they expect the problem to be solved on the first contact.
- They expect little or no wait time to reach a representative.
- In business-to-consumer channels like QVC, they expect their product to arrive on time.
- They expect delivery accuracy—ship what I want where I want it to go. If a customer has a problem with a product, he or she expects generous returns and refund policies, and he or she expects these returns and refunds to be processed accurately and timely.
- Customers expect you to call them if there is a problem.
- They expect that the company will listen and act upon what they are being told.
- Customers want multiple ways to reach your company.
- They expect the company to stand behind its product if it fails to deliver what was promised.
- They expect to deal with a company that they can trust, that will keep its word.

How We Started Giving Them What They Want

Identifying the right customer-centric initiatives involved the entire company. Here's what we did:

- Wrote new training methods for CSRs
- Established senior-level involvement in customer service
- Offered customers multiple options to reach CSRs
- Used social networking Web sites
- Constantly revisited our customer service business model
- Made our returns policy quick, friendly, and pain free

We've given our CSRs virtual real-time access to superiors to handle immediate problems.

The Customer Council: Senior-Level Involvement

We believe that providing quality customer service is every department's responsibility. So to facilitate this idea, we created a concept that we call the Customer Council. It's essentially a cross-functional customer advocacy team composed of our CEO, chief merchandising officer, senior marketing staff, and key business leaders. The goal is to have a place in which the customers' voice gets heard. We discuss our key customer metrics and establish our top customer experience priorities. Then we plan on how to resolve them. A chief customer officer moderates the team. When we meet, we look at all the data gathered from our multichannel environment—phone, Web, blogs, and mobile phone. At these monthly meetings, we identify key customer issues that require senior-level response—those critical issues that our normal channels couldn't resolve. The meeting serves the dual purpose of solving customer problems and seamlessly connecting all departments to allow that to happen. It creates awareness of what those issues are, and lets us create clear, crisp resolution strategies.

Such a meeting also makes your CEO your strongest customer advocate; his or her presence sends your organization the message that hearing the customer's voice is a priority.

Our interdepartmental relationships weren't always this cozy. When we first embarked on improving customers' experience, other departments fussed loudly about changing how they operated.

It was only after the VOC research correlated repeat purchases to excellent service that the rest of the company got on board.

It was only after the VOC research correlated repeat purchases to excellent service that the rest of the company got on board.

Offering Customers Multiple Options to Reach CSRs

Like other companies, we've considered pushing all our service options exclusively to the Web rather than incurring the expense of servicing our customers via live representatives. But we said no. Why? Because this strategy can be shortsighted and ignores the importance of giving the customer choices for using your service. Remember: Customers have many preferences. Some like the phone, others the Web. Also, the vast majority of QVC customers are women, and many of these customers prefer human contact.

We had similar internal discussions when we introduced our interactive voice response unit (VRU) to our customers.

Most companies offer a VRU option and allow customers to opt out to a live agent. Through our research we learned the following:

- The 10 percent of our customer base who would use only a voice response unit and not a live representative loved the VRU.
- Another 10 percent of our customers would never use a voice response unit and wanted to use only the representatives. Indeed, this group of customers was hostile to the idea of

navigating through a voice response unit. Surprisingly, many customers, even today, simply won't use a VRU.

- The remaining customers used the VRU sometimes and the representatives other times.

So we started our VRU in a counterintuitive manner. We offered the customer the "option" of dialing the VRU directly or talking to a live agent. We actually provided two phone numbers, and it was a smart move. It sounds a bit silly now, but there is a very important concept that is equally important in a multichannel environment: provide the customer with "personalized options" or choices.

We found that a small percentage of customers prefer to use only the Web or use only the live rep. *A much higher percentage uses both.* When customers need an immediate resolution on complex transactions, they speak with a live representative, and when they need a simple transaction, they use the Web.

Of course, the costs of live representatives are significantly higher than the Web experience; however, it's always more expensive to lose the customer. And if you let the short-term savings rule your long-term decisions, that's what is going to happen.

The concept of choice, while intuitively clear and observable by the selection of products we provide our customers, somehow gets lost when we think about service. We think this is primarily because the cost of providing this service is evident while the cost for not providing it is hidden. This only serves to highlight the importance of VOC feedback; it must be listened to, and it must be driven daily into your operations.

Using Social Networking

The advent of social networking and community has made it more important for companies to be aware of how the world is receiving their brand message. Yesterday, when customers had a bad service experience, they told 20 people—today they tell thousands. So, at QVC, we monitor the social networking groups to make sure that our customers are satisfied. If they aren't, we find out why.

QVC is well represented in cyberspace. There are community forums that talk about QVC; our Web site lets customers talk about QVC; Facebook users exchange stories about QVC; and customers now tweet about QVC. Make no mistake: the penalty for not listening to the customer today is a lot steeper than it was in years past; similarly, the penalty for service failures becomes steeper in a social media environment, with more impact to your brand. You need to figure out how to tap into these community forums, and make sure you are being spoken about in a good way.

The penalty for not listening to the customer today is a lot steeper than it was in years past; similarly, the penalty for service failures becomes steeper in a social media environment, with more impact to your brand.

Social networking and communities move fast.

Get on board!

Recently a customer used our QVC.com community forums to post her disappointment about the appearance of an artificial Christmas tree that she had bought.

After we spotted the post, a supervisor from our customer care and effort team called the customer at home and ensured her that a satisfactory replacement would be sent in time for the holidays.

This time, the message that the customer wrote was quite different:

> I wanted to let you all know that the Q is making an effort and my faith is restored, I'm really glad because I really like QVC.

The story generated positive buzz on the forums.

Making the Returns Policy Quick, Friendly, and Pain Free

Best-in-class companies have returns policies that help build customer confidence in their product. Having a strategy to process the returns quickly and to reimburse the customer is a strategy that helps reduce effort and builds trust. When our organization began to focus on significantly reducing the number of days it took to get a return processed and to credit the customers' accounts, we found a few good things happened.

We reduced the number of customer service inquiries in the call center and on the Web by more than 20 percent. Also, our actions reduced the customer dissatisfaction comments from the community. Instead of hearing complaints that QVC was slow in processing its returns, we heard a very positive buzz about how quick and efficient we were. All reinforcing customer confidence and trust in the organization, wanting to do the right thing for them.

To Outsource or Insource Your Call Center: The Pros and Cons

There is a legitimate difference of opinion today about whether companies should outsource their call centers. The debate generally focuses on costs, control of the brand experience, quality of service, and the ability to scale centers for business growth. We considered outsourcing, but we ultimately decided to keep our call center internal for several reasons, a primary one being that we can have enormous call volume spikes. Most third parties need a steady state of volume on a consistent basis to deliver the service levels that we require.

Controlling the customer experience and our brand message have been key strategies since QVC's inception. There is a strong connection between the voice the customer hears on the phone and the program host that is demonstrating the product. The brand message and experience must be consistent. QVC strongly feels it must control the connection with the customer and integrate it with our business model. Frankly, the loss of that control frightened our marketing leadership team. In fact, we used the potential cost savings that could be gained by using an outside vendor as a challenge to improve operations productivity, minimize the cost differences, and create better efficiencies.

When QVC was launched in 1986, more than 17 companies were broadcasting televised home shopping. Twenty-two years later, only 2 of those companies survive. What they have in common is that neither outsourced their broadcast, distribution, or customer service operations.

It is relevant too that none of the recent National Retail Federation Foundation/American Express 2009 Customers' Choice award winners outsourced their customer service. We believe much of this has to do with ensuring that there is an intimate knowledge of your product offerings and services as well as an intimate connection between the business and those employees who are delivering the service.

The Takeaways

Here is a list of action items that can help you with your Voice-of-the-Customer research and devise strategies that will improve your service:

- Create frequent VOC tracking surveys using the phone, e-mail, and Web sites. Benchmark how effective the customers feel you are against the metrics you've created. Watch your progress, or lack thereof, after implementing solutions. Capture customer preferences for products and services. Produce daily and weekly "product and/or service alert" reports to inform the organization of what customers really loved and what they disliked either due to damage, defect, poor quality, or late delivery.
- Include customer recommendations on new products, sizes, colors, and categories they want to see on the Internet, air, and phone.
- Create a Customer Council; make sure senior management is part of it.
- Create a culture of quick response to customers' requests, sending a thank you card or call when possible. Recognize and reward employees who provide great service and who are responsive to their customers.

- Educate all employees about customer research, highlighting the top challenges. Create cross-functional teams including operations, marketing, and finance, as well as merchandising teams, to solve them.
- Restructure customer service representatives' training and systems to respond to customer needs better.
- Conduct regular customer roundtables with call center employees to identify ways of improving customer satisfaction by serving the customer more efficiently.
- Create "end-to-end" customer scorecard metrics that tie the call centers, the Internet, mobile, the distribution centers, quality assurance, and merchandising together with overall accountability for improving things like product ratings and reviews, product satisfaction, and quality.
- Use your CSRs to help you sell and serve. They are the links to your customers.
- Let your CSRs capture customer comments and feed them to you. Targeting this information around key products is particularly important. However, it's critical that you create a feedback loop to the representatives not only thanking them for their input but also letting them know that the information received led to improved customer experience.
- Make sure everybody is learning about customers from your call centers. Get the senior leadership team in the loop, and make sure they can hear what customers think and say. Make sure the new recruits hear this too.
- Conduct customer surveys every two years.

Here's the bottom line: We have found that by reducing customer wait time, providing customers with the information that they need to buy the product, and making buying fun and simple are all critical deliverables for our customers. As a result, our percentage of repeat customers continues to rise.

The easier we make it for customers to do business with us, the cheaper it is for our bottom line and the more it increases repeat business. Indeed, a key metric for QVC is measuring the customer's ease of doing business. We find that when that number drops down, our costs increase. We believe that this concept is rooted in the total quality principles of the past: build it and do it right the first time and then watch the total cost of providing quality drop down.

Strong marketing organizations that are customer-centric understand the powerful effect the customers' experience, either negative or positive, has on the bottom line. We spent years learning about the impact of customer loyalty—defined as customer satisfaction plus repeat purchases and friend recommendation—on our bottom line. The better we understood it, the more clear it was to us that customer service is very much a marketing issue—one that can't be left only to the operations staff.

The customer's service experience does indeed have a profound impact on your sales and marketing efforts. It's our belief that great customer service should be everyone's job, including the marketing department's. Indeed, we hold the belief at QVC that great service is a competitive advantage that creates "customer stickiness," reinforcing the company's promise and generating customer loyalty.

NOW WHAT?

Follow QVC's example!

- Reposition service as a competitive advantage that creates "customer stickiness," reinforcing the company's value proposition and generating customer loyalty.
- Evangelize the VOC-driven customer service process with everyone in your organization, including senior management.
- Set up a Customer Council. Get senior-level involvement!

- Remember that great customer service should be everyone's job, including the marketing department's.
- Create multiple VOC input points. These should include face-to-face or phone interviews, tracking surveys, e-mail contact, and Web site feedback. Benchmark how effective the customers feel you are against the metrics you've created. Watch your progress (or lack thereof) after implementing possible solutions to the challenges customers identify.
- Create "end-to-end" customer scorecard metrics that tie the call centers, the Internet, mobile, the distribution centers, quality assurance, and merchandising together with overall accountability for improving things like product ratings and reviews, product satisfaction, and quality.
- Start measuring, comparing, and internally publicizing transition rates. If traditional response rates from one stage to another—say, suspect to prospect—have been 2 percent, implementing VOC-driven customer service initiatives can make that rate 10 percent. Once you identify an initiative that shows measurable improvement in one of these ratios, make sure people in your organization know about it!
- Make the case that *excellent service correlates statistically to repeat business.*

You're nearly across the finish line! In the next chapter, you'll learn how your organization can pass the final VOC test.

CHAPTER

11

THE FINAL VOC TEST: SUPERIOR CUSTOMER SERVICE

EXECUTIVE SUMMARY

- The way prospects and customers feel they have been treated by your company is the final, and best, test of whether your organization has in fact built itself around the Voice of the Customer.
- A VOC-driven customer service strategy will quickly transform how customers perceive your organization.
- Great customer service generates powerful commentary that circulates quickly through social media. So does poor customer service!
- At the end of the day, companies don't change because of data. They change because of VOC stories, especially customer service stories.

I had bought an electric baseboard heater from Home Depot in January 2008 for the amount of $37. When I tried to use it in October 2008, it would not work. I called the store and [learned] there was only a 90-day warranty on the heater. I called the distribution center to see if there was a recall on the heater. I gave them all the information needed and was called within three days and was told I would receive a $50 gift card in place of the heater. The gift card was rushed via UPS.

—An enthusiastic posting about a problem that turned into a solution for a Home Depot customer. The story was widely circulated on the Internet.

Questions to consider:

- Was the gift card a marketing tactic or a customer service tactic?
- How much more will the customer buy from Home Depot in coming years?
- How many people has the customer shared this story with via the Internet?
- How much goodwill did Home Depot realize by sending the gift card via UPS?
- How easy would it have been to apologize to this customer and explain that "there's nothing we can do"?
- *What would have been lost had Home Depot done that?*

SOBERING STATISTICS MARKETERS SHOULD READ AT LEAST ONCE A MONTH

- 68 percent of customer defection takes place because customers feel poorly treated.

  Source: www.CustomerServiceManager.com

- 91 percent of unhappy customers will not willingly do business with you again.
- 70 percent of complaining customers will do business with you again if you resolve the complaint in their favor.

- 95 percent of complaining customers will do business with you again if you resolve the complaint instantly.

  Source: Lee Resources, Inc.

- A typical business hears from only about 4 percent of its dissatisfied customers.
- 96 percent simply go away without complaining.
- Of those, 91 percent will never come back.

  Source: Ruby Newell-Legner, "Understanding Customers"

When we get to the heart of the matter, we are left with the momentous question, *how do customers feel?*

The way prospects and customers feel they have been treated by your organization is the final, and best, test of whether your organization has in fact built itself around the Voice of the Customer. If that voice is taken into account, your organization will likely get a second chance, even if there has been a serious problem. The next point may be familiar by now—we certainly hope it is—but it bears repeating: if that voice is ignored, your organization will not only lose its second chance but it will also create "negative evangelists," a scary scenario in this social media era.

WHO CAN AFFORD THAT?

Improving your organization's customer service by synchronizing it with the Voice of the Customer can improve your other marketing initiatives, transform your relationships with customers and prospects, energize your public relations efforts, and reposition your entire organization for maximum competitive advantage. If you're looking for a way to change the game in a hurry, you need look no further than your organization's relationship with its own prospects and customers.

Consider the remarkable recent achievements of a company operating in an industry that has long had a reputation for being indifferent to customers—the cable television industry.

CASE STUDY: COMCAST

CLOSE-UP ON COMCAST

- Founded in 1963
- Headquarters: Philadelphia, Pennsylvania
- Largest cable operator and largest Internet service provider in the United States
- Approximately 100,000 employees

Frank Eliason Tweets His Way to a Turnaround at Comcast

Frank Eliason, whom *BusinessWeek* has called the most famous customer service manager in America, is Comcast's director of digital care. He has won renown by implementing an idea that a few years ago would have seemed impossible: we should respond to customer complaints in minutes or seconds, rather than days or weeks.

The tool he's used to do this—Twitter—has made it possible for Comcast to begin the process of improving communication, and perceptions, with its huge customer base. Not coincidentally, it has also given Comcast a human face: Eliason's.

"The month after I started work here," he told us, "we got word that someone had started a little Web site called I HATE COMCAST. Senior management took that pretty seriously, and we decided that we had to make some changes. I made the case that one of those changes should be doing a better job of listening to customers one-on-one than we had been doing up to that point. Twitter has certainly been a big part of that change."

The online rants haven't disappeared entirely, but Comcast's impressive instant-response initiative via Twitter has certainly balanced them out with plenty of I LOVE COMCAST moments.

"We started a whole new listening initiative at Comcast, using social media," says Eliason. "We were using it for PR and marketing already; the goal now was to use the same tools to spot and interact with people who were complaining online. We wanted to listen to them, try to solve their problems, and, just as important, learn from them."

Spreading the Word

Eliason is quick to point out that much of what he has been able to accomplish has been a matter of engaging both customers and senior executives at Comcast with what he's hearing online from customers. "Once you have a story to tell or a clear, individualized customer to present," he has observed, "you can make the case for changing something internally that will improve the customer experience. If you don't have that story, you find it harder to change processes. Twitter has given us a way to communicate in real time with people, and it's also given us a lot of important stories to share internally."

He shares a story from early in his own career to illustrate the point: "A while back, I was working at a bank, and I was making a presentation to senior management about some changes I wanted to make to the policies the bank was expecting the front-line people to follow, policies that were hurting us with customers. I got nowhere because my presentation was all about the data. Technically, I had proved my point, but I hadn't inspired any action or any buy-in. A year later, I made the same points but with a different presentation. This time, instead of just citing numbers, I was able to play audio of the actual discussions that customers were having with our call center representatives. Instantly, I got attention and buy-in from senior management, and we were able to change the policies."

The Takeaways

The lesson? According to Eliason, it's pretty clear: the more specific you can get about what customers are actually experiencing, the easier it will be for senior people to feel the pain the customer is actually feeling, and the better you will be at creating the coalition for change within your organization. "We were able to change that policy within a week," he recalled. "It had been a point of pain for years, but it was only after we were able to get top management to hear the calls that the organization actually addressed the problem. *At the end of the day, companies don't change because of data. They change because of VOC stories.*

"What we're doing now at Comcast is replicating what we were able to do for the bank. Identifying actual pain points, fixing what we can on the spot, and, when we come across things we can't fix, sharing stories with top management and catalyzing change within the organization. When you can connect a key decision maker to the true story of a customer who's in pain, you can bring about change. Not before—at least not at a large organization. That's what listening really means, and many companies think they are listening to customers better than they actually are.

"Let's say that, after work, one of your employees comes across a friend on Facebook who's having some kind of service issue. What happens? Usually your employees do nothing. That's a culture problem. They should want to do something. You want a company culture where your own employees are committed to helping people to resolve the problem or get the right things done. If that's not the case, then you know the culture needs attention. A culture shift is going to have to happen. That type of culture's going to be extremely important in this new age because customers are much more powerful than they were before." (A side note: You'll find some advice on how to deal with such problems in Chapter 12 of this book.)

"In recent years, there's been a merging of the customer service function with PR and marketing, and I think that's a healthy trend. It's happening because all three of those disciplines now demand real-time conversations with people. Lots of traditional marketing initiatives launched through social media have failed. Why have they failed? Because marketers have tried to dictate what was going to happen next, or they send exactly the same message to lots of people simultaneously. That's not the same as engaging the customer in conversation. Think of the customer who has a problem: you may not always be able to solve the problem, but you can always have a conversation, and if the conversation plays out in the customer's chosen arena, in the customer's preferred time frame, which is usually 'right now,' you may be able to change the way people feel about your organization."

At the end of the day, companies don't change because of data. They change because of VOC stories.

—FRANK ELIASON,
DIRECTOR OF DIGITAL CARE, COMCAST

Thanks to Eliason, a Comcast-friendly Twitter network now exists—one in which customers actually help each other out with the occasional problem and share quick-resolution success stories about how the act of posting a complaint tweet brought an almost instant response from the cable giant.

A HAPPY COMCAST CUSTOMER

Last year I bought Comcast's NBA League Pass, . . . I asked my brother if he wanted it again this year, and he said that he didn't really want to shell out the money for it, so I could go ahead and cancel it if I wasn't going to use it. . . . I casually explained to the Comcast rep that I wanted to cancel League Pass this year since I wasn't going to use it. She put me on hold so she could pull up my account. After a few minutes she came back and cheerfully informed me that I couldn't cancel my subscription since the NBA season had already started. . . . While I had been chatting with Not At All Helpful Comcast Rep on the phone, I happened to Twitter the following:

I hate Comcast.

To my surprise, after I hung up and was gearing up to unleash some major Comcast hate all over the Internet, I received this response [from ComcastBill]:

What's the issue?

I responded to ComcastBill in three tweets, relaying what had happened within the confines of 140 characters. Meanwhile, a number of my Twitter buddies rallied in support of my cause. . . . After some back-and-forths with ComcastBill, I gave him my account information, and he was quiet for a bit. After a while, he privately messaged me with this:

Don't worry about it;
we are crediting $170 to your account.

Needless to say, I was once again a happy happy Comcast customer.

—Post via seomoz.org

ANOTHER VOICE IN SUPPORT OF REAL-TIME CUSTOMER SERVICE

It's very easy for people on the outside of a company or an organization to see you as a monolith. You're a corporate entity, or you're a building, or you're a logo, or you're this giant chain of stores, when really we're a whole bunch of laid-back people with pretty idealistic visions of what we want to do. . . . I feel like social media networking is falling into buckets right now where people are using it for sales and marketing, people are using it for customer service, or people are using it to establish a corporate personality and corporate culture.

[O]ur number-one focus on Twitter is customer service. [We're] directly responding to people who have questions. They'll ask us, "Can I get this at my local store?" or "What are your holiday hours going to be?" or "Can you tell me a gluten-free alternative to corn-bread stuffing?"

I definitely think that people who tweet on behalf of an organization need to be in it. If you can find the wonderful combination of someone who really knows your business and really knows social media, then that's the person to use, even if he or she is in the meat department or is a cashier.

—Marla Erwin, Interactive Art Director for Whole Foods
Market, which now boasts over 1.75 million Twitter
followers and is the single most popular retailer on Twitter

(Interviewed in SocialMediaExaminer.com, February 9, 2010)

CASE STUDY:
1-800-FLOWERS GROWS AND GROWS, THANKS TO CUSTOMER FEEDBACK

CLOSE-UP ON 1-800-FLOWERS
- Founded in 1976
- Headquarters: Carle Place, New York
- Specializes in retail sales of flowers and gifts within the United States

- Among the earliest retailers to offer consumers a toll-free telephone number 24 hours a day, 7 days a week; later, an innovator in online and social media marketing
- Approximately 4,000 employees
- www.1800flowers.com

Superior customer service is possible only when top leadership believes in the principle of engaging directly with the customer. In a recent discussion, Chris McCann, CEO of the pioneering retailer 1-800-Flowers, emphasized the strategic importance of engaging, staying close to, and listening to his customers. Here's what he had to say:

"From its earliest days, this company has been founded on the principle of building the relationship first, and doing business second. That goes not only for our customers but for employees and for all of our other stakeholders. There have been a lot of opportunities over the past couple of years when we've been able to use things like the Internet and social media to follow through on this critical organizational priority of building relationships. One of the things I'm proudest of has been launching our own customer panel. This group got its start when I asked for the e-mail addresses of our very best customers. I then e-mailed each of them, and I basically asked each one for his or her help.

"I said, 'I'm looking for something—a group that I can turn to when I have questions. I'll never send you a form or a poll to fill out because I don't like surveys. What I will do from time to time is hit you with a question or two and ask for your insights and opinions. You'll also have full access to me. You can offer me suggestions at any time, just by picking up the phone and calling me. Would you agree to do this?'

"People said 'yes,' and suddenly we had a customer panel. One of the first issues was choosing a name. I said, 'Here are a couple of things we could call this group.' What we settled on, with their feedback, was 'Chris's Exchange.'

"Chris's Exchange has become a flexible resource that has helped our business a lot. When I have an idea for a new product or service, I share it with the group. Sometimes, an idea I share internally will get only a mediocre response from the people who work here; then, when I share the same idea with Chris's Exchange, I may get an overwhelmingly powerful response. That's important information. You have to be careful, of course, because every group has its biases. But this particular group of customers has given me a barometer I can use to get important feedback before I make major decisions."

McCann's penchant for engaging the customer in innovative ways extends to virtually all aspects of the business. A recent social media initiative, for instance, has been to issue Facebook reminders to 1-800-Flowers customers about the upcoming birthdays of friends and loved ones!

CASE STUDY:
THE DISNEY STANDARD—BLURRING THE LINES

We saved the last word on the transforming, game-changing power of superior customer service for one of the acknowledged world-class leaders in the field: The Walt Disney Companies. Scott Hudgins, whom you met in a previous chapter, gave us this detailed—and memorable—answer to the question, "How do the Disney destinations maintain their sterling reputation for extraordinary service?" Here's what he told us:

"My role is a marketing role, but if I were to ask my senior leadership what they're holding me accountable for, it would be repeat visitation. That changes your mindset. Every single interaction with a guest affects that goal. So when you realize that that's what you're really trying to accomplish, you start to move away from the mindset that says, How can I convert this into a sale? You start focusing instead on the question, How can I create a long-term relationship with this person?

"That leads to a whole lot of related questions. For instance, Can I get the person to have a good enough experience with us that, without our having to do anything else, he or she is going to want to come back? And: What might prevent that kind of experience from happening? How could we plan things so that that good experience is repeatable with other guests? The emphasis on repeat visitation makes you take on a service-oriented mindset, and more importantly, an experience-oriented mindset, across every interaction.

"When you get right down to it, we're in the business of creating unique, immersive experiences. Whenever and however we can do that,

that's our mission. That standard affects absolutely everything we do. Obviously, there are practical needs you have to take into account. But you start with that mindset of wanting each interaction to contribute to the experience as a whole. You begin with the overall result of wanting guests to feel like they got enough value out of this trip to come back without your even having to reach out to them again. When you start from that point, what you find is that not only does what you're doing blur the line between customer service and operations but it also blurs all the lines. You realize that everything is interconnected. Sales, service, one business unit versus the other, food and beverage versus merchandise, call center versus online—you name it.

"If it touches the prospective guest, it's going to affect that guest's experience, and it is going to affect that guest's desire to come back for a second time. So we're constantly asking ourselves: *How do we make sure the practical experiences match up with the emotional and content experiences? How do we make sure everything lines up and supports a single compelling story for the guest, a story that he or she wants to hear again?*

"Getting all the people who interact with the guest to buy into that view, and act in accordance with it, is part of the Disney legacy. It's something we see as a central part of the company culture. When you begin working for Disney, you know that you are taking part in something special that you as an individual want to be a part of, and you are consistently treated in a manner that lets you know that you and your contributions are valued. The result is that we have very high-quality product offering and an unwavering focus on the guest. We know that it's important to take the time to stay true to our heritage. Not everyone gets to work for an organization that goes all the way back to Walt Disney, and the ideals and principles he put forward. We do get to work at that company, and that's an honor. The importance of our company's legacy is something every cast member gets some very powerful, emotional exposure to from very early on. People have a sense of purpose behind that. We are all playing a part in a show that has a meaningful impact on people's lives.

"Now, I realize that not every company can appeal directly to the legacy of a Walt Disney, but I think every company can, and should, find elements from its own history and its best leadership that give employees a sense of engagement and purpose. That's a critical early step in creating a positive experience for the customer."

Do what you do so well that they will want to see it again and bring their friends.

—WALT DISNEY

NOW WHAT?

- Remember: Superior customer service can significantly change the game—both with an individual customer and within the market as a whole.
- Share compelling customer stories with top management to win attention to areas where your organization needs to improve. *"At the end of the day, companies don't change because of data. They change because of VOC stories."*
- Use Twitter and other methods to keep track of what customers and prospects are saying about your organization online.
- Respond quickly to online complaints, even if you don't have an instant solution.
- Get your people to believe that their goal is not to close a sale but to win an *ongoing relationship with the customer.*
- Ask yourself: Is your service good enough to create a desire to do business with your organization again?
- Instill in your frontline employees the sense of engagement, purpose, and commitment necessary to build high-value relationships. If, during "off hours," team members are not willing to address, or even note, a customer's problem with your organization, that's a sign of a larger cultural problem. (You'll find some strategies for dealing with such problems in Chapter 12.)

Perhaps you're wondering, "How do I get my organization to accept and implement the ideas I've learned about in this book?" You'll find out in the next chapter.

12

ALIGNING THE ORGANIZATION FOR **VOC** CHANGE

EXECUTIVE SUMMARY

- The VOC Relationship Marketing Process requires organizational change. That is not easy. Begin by asking key stakeholders: "Whom do you serve?"
- For the total organization to listen to the Voice of the Customer, all entities of the organization must support each other and must determine who their internal or external clients are.
- The critical key performance indicator that measures success in serving the respective customer is *repeat purchases*.
- Other key performance indicators (KPIs), specific to your industry and experience, must also be developed and monitored. More KPI examples appear in the Appendix.

One common question from managers who learn about the five VOC Relationship Marketing Process steps I've shared in this book is this: *How do I align an entire organization with the Voice of the Customer?*

Another question is just as important: *What are the key performance indicators I should measure to determine whether what we're doing is actually working?*

I posed both questions to legendary author and management consultant Dr. Ichak Adizes, founder and CEO of the Adizes Institute. His responses were so compelling and so concisely stated that I decided to devote this chapter to them.

THE VOICE OF THE CUSTOMER AND
ORGANIZATIONAL GROWTH

"Think of your organization as a living thing, an organism. You cannot have only the outer part, the skin of the organization—the client interface, or the marketing department, or the sales department, or the help desk—be the only part of the body that absorbs the Voice of the Customer. If information from the customer never penetrates to any other part of the organization, it won't act in accordance with what the customer is telling you.

"The question is, how do you take that VOC information throughout the organization, so that it can deal with the customer correctly at all levels?

"The answer, I believe, lies in changing the internal dynamic of the organization, and the best way to begin that is by changing the vocabulary. I emphasize the term *client* to make the point that we all must serve somebody. If we used the word *customer*, usually it would apply only to the sales or marketing department, and that is not enough.

"It's true: not everyone can be listening to or reporting to an end user. That end user, that customer, is just one kind of client. Many clients are internal. And every manager, every employee, every unit of the organization, large or small, must have a client to serve. By serving each other, the customer can be served well, and his or her voice be well heard.

"Again, look at any organism. Each part of the body exists in order to serve something else. The heart has a client—its client is the rest of the organization, and its service is the job of circulating blood. The lungs have a client—they must circulate oxygen to the bloodstream. The only thing that doesn't have a client, and that serves only itself, is a cancer.

"If there is a cancer in the organization, if there is something that doesn't serve anybody else, then we know the outcome of that situation. The organization starts dying.

"Once everybody within the enterprise has somebody to serve, once everybody starts organizing the day and the week and the quarter around the idea of service to some specific client, then internalizing the Voice of the Customer within the organization as a whole becomes a realizable goal.

"Let's say that marketing is listening the most intently to the Voice of the Customer, and it is following the five steps laid out in this book. The question to ask isn't, 'How can marketing share what it knows?' The better question is, 'Who serves marketing?' It is sales, and who should be serving sales well? Clearly it's production. Similarly, logistics is serving production, and human resources is serving logistics. And if all units serve each other well, the organization is going to internalize important messages and priorities that align with the Voice of the Customer.

"Before long, each of these elements is asking, 'What do the people I am serving need?' Before long, you have everybody serving somebody else. When you have everybody serving somebody else, you have a healthy body. The organization as a whole has internalized the most critical parts of the message. The major obstacle to this is the organizational cancer that arises when one unit or work group says:

- 'We don't have to serve anyone.'
- Or: 'We have all the other units to serve us.'
- Or, perhaps most common: 'We serve, but we do so on our own terms; our own needs take precedence over anyone else's needs; we don't have to listen to anyone's needs.'

"Such a group can impede healthy growth and adaptation, and literally kill the enterprise. That is where true leadership is required when it comes to implementing the Voice of the Customer: identifying cancer and healing it by requesting it to identify its clients and its needs and serving those clients well before it can damage and destroy the entire organization. If any unit is nonresponsive, it is time to replace its management.

"If someone in your organization can't or won't answer the question, 'Whom do you serve?' then it's time to check for cancer. If the tumor stays the same or gets worse, then it's time to cut it out."

THE ONE KEY PERFORMANCE INDICATOR TO WATCH

"The single most important key performance indicator (KPI) for an organization that is trying to implement the VOC principles outlined in this book is *repeat purchases*. Note, however, that purchase usually entails payment. That is relatively easy to identify through revenue. In the case of clients who are internal and usually do not pay for services, we must still find out whether the unit is effective. In these cases, we ask, 'If the clients had a choice, would they COME BACK?'

"If the repeat-business metric is trending upward, you may rest assured you are on the right track. If that metric is trending downward, you have a problem somewhere.

"A metric that can mislead you about how well you are doing in building your business around the Voice of the Customer is *profit.*

"Profit is the *result* of listening efficiently to the Voice of the Customer. It does not measure by itself the effectiveness of listening to the customer. It's too volatile, and too prone to manipulation. A company can increase profits by listening less to the Voice of the Customer and by cutting services. In the short run, it will be more profitable, but it could well go broke in the long run."

The points raised by Dr. Adizes are profoundly important. They should help you achieve the cross-functional linkages necessary to bring about the transformational changes we have been discussing. Imagine every group in the organization serving another group—all guided by the common goal of better serving the customers, per their VOC preferences.

> You'll find in the Appendix a summary of other key performance indicators monitored by contributors to this book.

NOW WHAT?

Consider the words of Steve Ballmer, CEO of Microsoft, who once observed: "We can believe that we know where the world should go. But unless we're in touch with our customers, our model of the world can diverge from reality. There's no substitute for innovation, of course, but innovation is no substitute for being in touch either."

As a final point of value for you, in the Epilogue, I've summarized the most important lessons this book has to offer about listening to, and following, the Voice of the Customer. I hope you will use this as your summary of key VOC takeaways.

SUMMARY OF THE KEY VOC TAKEAWAYS

Thank you for having invested the time to read this book. I hope it has delivered what it promised. I hope also that you now have both the passion and the guidelines for transforming your company's marketing.

I'm often asked to summarize the VOC process into a few easy-to-remember points. These are those points, and they are the major take-aways I would like you to keep in mind:

1. The customer is at the center of your universe. You have to keep earning the right to remain in his or her orbit of relevance.
2. You will not understand how customers define relevance and value *until and unless you ask them*! It is arrogant to presume that you know this because you know what they bought, why they

bought it, what some data overlay indicates, and so on. Making these assumptions is a poor replacement for understanding how we can engage meaningfully with our customers. Remember, if assumptions about what you think you know about the customer were sufficient, you would already be achieving double-digit response rates.

3. Trust the Five Step Relationship Marketing Process. It has been refined over the course of decades. It is a proven process, one that is both repeatable and scalable.

Those, then, are my Big Three Takeaways. I should probably add a fourth: The Golden Rule. In the end, you will find that, if you treat your customer with the same respect you yourself would want to experience as a customer of your organization, you will get all the guidance you need.

As a final point of value for you, I've prepared a summary of the most important lessons this book has to offer about listening to, and following, the Voice of the Customer. I hope you will use this as your summary of the key VOC takeaways.

STEP 1.
CONDUCT AND APPLY VOC RELATIONSHIP RESEARCH

- Focus on the customer experience.
- Customers and members of your community must feel a true connection with your organization; this must constantly be reinforced.
- As you consider the potential of the VOC Research Process to increase sales or repeat purchases, think about using the VOC research to accomplish the following:
  o Generate an in-depth understanding of the value customers expect from your company, throughout the major points in their life cycle of experience with your company.
  o Identify gaps between the customers' brand expectation and their actual experience with your organization.
  o Understand how to establish and maintain relevance across your multiple channels and points of contact.

○ Determine the effectiveness of your media mix. Are customers getting too many communications, and with not enough relevance?

○ Identify how you can better personalize the customer experience, whether online, in person, or over the phone.

STEP 2.
CREATE VOC-DRIVEN OPT-IN RELATIONSHIP STRATEGIES

Opt-in is about engaging customers to take an active role in defining the relationship—per their needs. This enables us to understand how we can be relevant to them at an *individual level*: right message, right offer, sent to the right people, at the right time, and via their medium of choice. This information will then form our uniquely powerful and accurate opt-in preference database.

• Make sure the value of opting in to a relationship with your organization is obvious and differentiated.
• Personalize the experience according to the unique self-profiling information of the customer.
• Find ways to remind the user how you are customizing his or her experience.
• Don't promise value during the opt-in process that you can't deliver because the penalty for not delivering once you have raised expectations can be huge.
• Keep the customer engaged after the initial contact—otherwise, the data you have collected will quickly become irrelevant, and the relationship will die.

Make sure your opt-in program adheres to these six principles, via Peppers and Rogers:

1. Use a flexible opt-in policy.
2. Make it clear and simple.
3. Establish a value exchange.
4. Tread cautiously with targeted Web ads.
5. Create a culture of customer trust.
6. Remember: You're responsible for your partners too.

STEP 3.
CREATE A VOC-DRIVEN MULTICHANNEL MIX

Implement these six multichannel requirements for the new millennium:

1. The optimal deployment of media should be driven by VOC learnings to ensure both relevance and effectiveness.
2. Key elements of the multichannel mix must be deployed per the individual opt-in preferences of customers and prospects.
3. The multichannel mix must provide customers and prospects with choices so they can communicate with the marketer via the media mix of their choice.
4. The channel mix must perform items 1 through 3 above in accordance with the timing and frequency determined by that individual's opt-in preferences.
5. The channel mix must offer a completely integrated experience. All the elements must complement each other, support each other, and send coordinated messages to customers and prospects.
6. The channel mix must be responsive. If the organization alienates or abuses a consumer, you can expect to hear about it in a public forum if you do not resolve it privately.
   o Identify innovative multichannel initiatives that engage customers in new ways and across many parts of their life cycle and lifestyle.
   o Place more importance on being interested than on being interesting.
   o Engage locally. This is the only reliable way to beat worldwide brands.
   o Individualize multichannel communication with consumers and key allies.
   o Consider creating alliances with key players in your consumers' support network; these relationships may create new, competitively differentiating channels for you.
   o Build a multichannel strategy that supports your opt-in strategy. Collect only the information that will be used to drive relevant and personally useful information and/or resources to customers.

STEP 4.
CREATE A VOC-DRIVEN SOCIAL MEDIA PRESENCE

- Consider using VOC research to understand how customers and prospects define a deeper, ongoing relationship with your company and how that should be experienced via social media.
- Find out where your customers and prospects are going to discuss your company and other related firms. Listen, learn, and participate in the dialogue if appropriate.
- Personalize your message, and keep it authentic.
- Make it easy for people to leave their mark.
- Build loyalty through *engagement*. People who participate in an effective online community return to a site nine times as often and five times as long.
- Try to weed out the impersonal, transactional, or generic customer experiences so they don't cause customers and prospects to feel that they cannot connect with your organization, express preferences, and experience the promised brand experience.
- Harness the power of narrative. Tell a story about your organization or someone connected to it.
- Forget about the hard sell. Focus instead on connection and conversation.
- Personalize, personalize, personalize: strive to provide prospects and customers information and resources that are directly relevant to their lives.
- Synchronize PR and social media. Send the same core message through all channels.
- Target effectively, and respond quickly to everyone you target. Once you identify your customer, the relationship is precious. Follow through promptly on the conversation with that person—and remember that social media has turned customer response time expectations into minutes and hours, not days or weeks.
- Give your people access to the social media tools they need to do the job.
- Focus on creating and supporting conversations with engaged members of your audience—a vastly different goal than just "selling" prospects your products and services.

- Create and support an engaged community of fans.
- Learn all you can about the "crowdsourcing" business model. The implications on engaging your community of customers may be profound.
- View SEO and SEM as a numbers-driven science that allows you to target consumers effectively and to capture the Voice of the Customer in real time.
- Use social media to demonstrate transparency, accountability, and mission commitment to your critical stakeholders—and everyone else.
- Encourage people to follow individual personalities who are strongly associated with your organization's mission.

STEP 5.
INVEST IN AN EXCELLENT CUSTOMER SERVICE EXPERIENCE

- Reposition service as a competitive advantage that creates "customer stickiness," reinforcing the company's value proposition and generating customer loyalty.
- Evangelize the VOC-driven customer service process with everyone in your organization, including senior management.
- Set up a Customer Council. Get senior-level involvement!
- Remember that great customer service should be everyone's job, including the marketing department's.
- Create multiple VOC input points. These should include face-to-face or phone interviews, tracking surveys, e-mail contact, and Web site feedback. Benchmark how effective the customer feels you are against the metrics you've created. Watch your progress (or lack thereof) after implementing possible solutions to the challenges customers identify.
- Create "end-to-end" customer scorecard metrics that tie the call centers, the Internet, mobile, the distribution centers, quality assurance, and merchandising together with the overall accountability for improving things like product ratings and reviews, product satisfaction, and quality.
- Start measuring, comparing, and internally publicizing transition rates. If traditional response rates from one stage to another—say,

suspect to prospect—have been 2 percent, implementing VOC-driven customer service initiatives can make that rate 10 percent. Once you identify an initiative that shows measurable improvement in one of these ratios, make sure people in your organization know about it!

- Make the case that excellent service correlates statistically to repeat business.
- Remember: Superior customer service can significantly change the game—both with an individual customer and within the market as a whole.
- Share compelling customer stories with top management to win attention to areas where your organization needs to improve. "At the end of the day, companies don't change because of data. They change because of VOC stories."
- Use Twitter and other methods to keep track of what customers and prospects are saying about your organization online.
- Respond quickly to online complaints, even if you don't have an instant solution.
- Get your people to believe that their goal is not to "close a sale" but to win an ongoing relationship with the customer.
- Ask yourself: Is your service good enough to create a desire to do business with your organization again?
- Make sure everyone in your organization knows the answer to the question "Whom do you serve?"

Please drop me a line at ErnanRoman@erdm.com. We want to stay in touch with you for three reasons. First, so we can share the latest learnings about the art and science of pursuing the wisdom of the customer. Second, so we can learn from you about what you experienced personally as a result of reading this book. And third, so we can keep our own model of the world from diverging too far from reality.

We look forward to hearing from you!

Appendix

Key Performance Indicators

In addition to the important *repeat purchase metric* cited by Dr. Adizes in Chapter 12, other key performance indicators specific to your industry and experience must be developed and monitored. We asked some of the contributors to this book to share their thoughts on the best key performance indicators and benchmarks to measure over time, and the best ways to support organizational change over time. Here are some of their responses.

Leslie Reiser

"Functionality and capability of the program will dictate the majority of key KPIs. However, there are a variety of core metrics that should always be included. Some of the KPI components we use include these:

- *Traffic:* Where are the majority of users coming from, and what are the key messages or actions that bring them to the experience? Knowing this information will help to ensure the appropriate target audience is being driven to and reaching the experience.
- *Unique visitors versus returning visitors:* What is the ratio?
- *Time on site:* Once customers arrive, how long do they remain? Including exit pages—where do users drop off?
- *Page views:* What is the average number of pages the users navigate to?
- *Engagement:* What action are users taking when they spend time on the site?
- *Conversions:* If the experience requires membership or offers purchasing options, what percentage of visitors convert?

"Well-chosen KPIs influence growth and strategy. They allow you to optimize your efforts and focus your attention on what works and what your core users need. The results gathered from the program KPIs should influence the future direction of the strategy.

"Poorly chosen KPIs are empty numbers. Traditionally, numbers are the primary focus to identifying success. But the reality of having huge numbers does not translate into success. Too often, marketers strive to achieve a 'collection' of users and/or clients to create a large audience, but if the desired engagement or action from the users is absent, the value of that 'collection' is minimal.

"Focus less on the numbers and more on the action of the clients. If you have 100,000 members, but only 100 engage, is that success? What if you only had 10,000 users, but 5,000 were engaged? Which would you rather have?"

—*Leslie Reiser, Program Director of Digital Marketing,*
WW General Business, IBM

Pernille Thorslund Kyhl

"For me, a well-chosen KPI is basic enough to be important and relevant over time even if other things change.

"Do not rely on a single source of consumer feedback. E-mails from consumers, for instance, may appear to magnify the 'yelling' of unsatisfied customers over the silence of satisfied ones."

—*Pernille Thorslund Kyhl, Nordic Consumer Relationship*
Marketing Manager, Libero, SCA Hygiene Products A/S

Frank Eliason

"In service, you can measure the number of interactions, but I prefer the benefits gained, such as changed processes, policies, or new solutions offered by customers. All these can be measured with financial benefits."

—*Frank Eliason, Senior Director,*
National Customer Operations, Comcast

Ole Stangerup

"We have developed a sequence of 14 questions covering all aspects of our delivery to customers, including timing, quality, the effectiveness of a single point of contact for resolving problems, and so on. These questions are asked in our customer satisfaction survey twice a year. We ask customers to rank us against the following elements on a scale of 1 to 5:

1. Quick delivery
2. Timely delivery
3. Flexibility
4. High quality, few errors
5. The ability to document value
6. Listens to my needs and acts accordingly
7. Understands my business and my needs
8. Proactiveness
9. Has a service-minded attitude
10. One point of contact
11. Delivers cross channels
12. Systems and/or platforms—width and depth
13. Inspires me
14. Sets the agenda in the industry

"These questions are asked in two ways:

1. How would you rank your own experience regarding . . . ?

"And then, after the consumer has responded about his or her personal experience with us for all the issues, we ask:

2. How important is this to you personally? (About the same 14 issues.)

"By doing this, we get a clear result on how we perform, connected with the importance of each of the 14 issues, as seen from the customer's point of view. The difference between the customer's experience with us and that issue's importance to the person tells us whether we are on track or not. Any area where we are two or more points below the customer's expectations is quickly highlighted, so the customer's contact person can follow up personally.

"The scores are all potential KPIs for different persons in our organization."

—*Ole Stangerup, Relationship Marketing Officer,*
Express A/S

Garry Dawson

"We measure on several dimensions:

1. *Customer feedback:* Examples are loyalty indexes, satisfaction ratings, and so forth. This is feedback directly from customers.
2. *Employee feedback:* Examples include engagement, satisfaction with management.
3. *Company and business results:* This includes revenue in terms of earnings per share (EPS) at the company level and share of wallet (SOW) at the account or group-of-accounts level within key accounts."

—Garry Dawson, Americas Advertising and Direct Marketing Manager, Hewlett-Packard

INDEX

ABOUT THE AUTHOR

Ernan Roman is president of the marketing consultancy Ernan Roman Direct Marketing (ERDM). He is one of the leading authorities in Voice of Customer–driven relationship marketing, and he was named to *BtoB*'s "Who's Who" as one of the "100 most influential people" in business marketing by Crain's *BtoB* magazine.

Roman is recognized as the industry pioneer who created three important methodologies: Integrated Direct Marketing, Opt-In Marketing, and Voice of Customer Relationship Research.

ERDM provides marketing consulting services for innovative Fortune and growth companies such as Microsoft, NBC Universal, Walt Disney, Reliant Energy, Hewlett-Packard, IBM, MSC Industrial Direct, and Songza Media, Inc.

Roman is the coauthor of *Opt-In Marketing: Increase Sales Exponentially with Consensual Marketing* and the author of *Integrated Direct Marketing: The Cutting-Edge Strategy for Synchronizing Advertising, Direct Mail, Telemarketing, and Field Sales.*

WANT MORE
GAME-CHANGING STRATEGIES
AND INSIGHTS?

Subscribe to Ernan Roman's free *Relationship Marketing Insights* newsletter and tap into the very latest about today's most successful marketing organizations. Learn how they're leveraging VOC insights to drive deeper levels of engagement, relevance, and revenue.

Each edition contains strategies, tips, and case studies to help you achieve consistent double-digit response through Voice-of-the-Customer marketing. Subscribe at www.erdm.com.

For answers to your questions about how to improve your relationship marketing and how to use Voice-of-the-Customer Research, e-mail Ernan Roman at ErnanRoman@erdm.com.